D0094918

DATE DUE

THE LIMITS OF REASON

RELIGIOUS PERSPECTIVES
Planned and Edited by
RUTH NANDA ANSHEN

BOARD OF EDITORS

W. H. Auden

Karl Barth

Martin C. D'Arcy

Christopher Dawson

C. H. Dodd

Mircea Eliade

Muhammad Zafrullah Khan

Alexandre Koyré

Jacques Maritain

James Muilenburg

Sarvepalli Radhakrishnan

Gershom Scholem

D. T. Suzuki

Paul Tillich

RELIGIOUS PERSPECTIVES • VOLUME THREE

THE LIMITS OF REASON

by George Boas

GREENWOOD PRESS, PUBLISHERS
NEW YORK   1968

THE LIMITS OF REASON
Copyright © 1961 by George Boas

Reprinted with the permission of
Harper & Row Publishers

LIBRARY OF CONGRESS catalogue card number: 68-21324

Printed in the United States of America

B
53
B56
1968

To **K.B.D.** and **W.F.D.**

with a father's love

YRP 12/9/70

CONTENTS

RELIGIOUS PERSPECTIVES

RELIGIOUS PERSPECTIVES
Its Meaning and Purpose

RELIGIOUS PERSPECTIVES represents a quest for the rediscovery of man. It constitutes an effort to define man's search for the essence of being in order that he may have a knowledge of goals. It is an endeavor to show that there is no possibility of achieving an understanding of man's total nature on the basis of phenomena known by the analytical method alone. It hopes to point to the false antinomy between revelation and reason, faith and knowledge, grace and nature, courage and anxiety. Mathematics, physics, philosophy, biology and religion, in spite of their almost complete independence, have begun to sense their interrelatedness and to become aware of that mode of cognition which teaches that "the light is not without but within me, and I myself am the light."

Modern man is threatened by a world created by himself. He is faced with the conversion of mind to naturalism, a dogmatic secularism and an opposition to a belief in the transcendent. He begins to see, however, that the universe is given not as one existing and one perceived but as the unity of subject and object; that the barrier between them cannot be said to have been dissolved as the result of recent experience in the physical sciences, since this barrier has never existed. Confronted with the question of meaning, he is summoned to rediscover and scrutinize the immutable and the permanent which constitute the dynamic, unifying aspect of life as well as the principle of differentiation; to reconcile identity and diversity, immutability and unrest. He begins to recognize that just as every person descends by his particular path, so he is able to ascend, and this ascent aims at a return to the source of creation, an inward home from which he has become estranged.

It is the hope of RELIGIOUS PERSPECTIVES that the rediscovery of man will point the way to the rediscovery of God. To this end a rediscovery of first principles should constitute part of the quest. These principles, not to be superseded by new discoveries, are not those of historical worlds that come to be and perish. They are to be sought in the heart and spirit of man, and no interpretation of a merely historical or scientific universe can guide the search. RELIGIOUS PERSPECTIVES attempts not only to ask dispassionately what the nature of God is, but also to restore

11

to human life at least the hypothesis of God and the symbols that relate to him. It endeavors to show that man is faced with the metaphysical question of the truth of religion while he encounters the empirical question of its effects on the life of humanity and its meaning for society. Religion is here distinguished from theology and its doctrinal forms and is intended to denote the feelings, aspirations and acts of men, as they relate to total reality.

RELIGIOUS PERSPECTIVES is nourished by the spiritual and intellectual energy of world thought, by those religious and ethical leaders who are not merely spectators but scholars deeply involved in the critical problems common to all religions. These thinkers recognize that human morality and human ideals thrive only when set in a context of a transcendent attitude toward religion and that by pointing to the ground of identity and the common nature of being in the religious experience of man, the essential nature of religion may be defined. Thus, they are committed to re-evaluate the meaning of everlastingness, an experience which has been lost and which is the content of that *visio Dei* constituting the structure of all religions. It is the many absorbed everlastingly into the ultimate unity, a unity subsuming what Whitehead calls the fluency of God and the everlastingness of passing experience.

These volumes will seek to show that the unity of which we speak consists in a certitude emanating from the nature of man who seeks God and the nature of God who seeks man. Such certitude bathes in an intuitive act of cognition, participating in the divine essence and is related to the natural spirituality of intelligence. This is not by any means to say that there is an equivalence of all faiths in the traditional religions of human history. It is, however, to emphasize the distinction between the spiritual and the temporal which all religions acknowledge. For duration of thought is composed of instants superior to time, and is an intuition of the permanence of existence and its metahistorical reality. In fact, the symbol* itself found on cover and jacket of each volume of RELIGIOUS PERSPECTIVES is the visible sign or representation of the essence, immediacy and timelessness of religious experience; the one immutable center, which may be analogically related to Being in pure act, moving with centrifugal and ecumenical necessity outward into the manifold modes, yet simulta-

* From the original design by Leo Katz.

neously, with dynamic centripetal power and with full intentional energy, returning to the source. Through the very diversity of its authors, the Series shows that the basic and poignant concern of every faith is to point to and overcome the crisis in our apocalyptic epoch—the crisis of man's separation from man and of man's separation from God—the failure of love. The authors endeavor, moreover, to illustrate the truth that the human heart is able, and even yearns, to go to the very lengths of God; that the darkness and cold, the frozen spiritual misery of recent time, are breaking, cracking and beginning to move, yielding to efforts to overcome spiritual muteness and moral paralysis. In this way, it is hoped, the immediacy of pain and sorrow, the primacy of tragedy and suffering in human life, may be transmuted into a spiritual and moral triumph.

RELIGIOUS PERSPECTIVES is therefore an effort to explore the *meaning* of God, an exploration which constitutes an aspect of man's intrinsic nature, part of his ontological substance. The Series grows out of an abiding concern that in spite of the release of man's creative energy which science has in part accomplished, this very science has overturned man's conception of the essential order of nature. Shrewd as man's calculations have become concerning his means, his choice of ends which was formerly correlated with belief in God, with absolute criteria of conduct, has become witless. God is not to be treated as an exception to metaphysical principles, invoked to prevent their collapse. He is rather their chief exemplification, the source of all potentiality. The personal reality of freedom and providence, of will and conscience, may demonstrate that "he who knows" commands a depth of consciousness inaccessible to the profane man, and is capable of that transfiguration which prevents the twisting of all good to ignominy. This religious content of experience is not within the province of science to bestow; it corrects the error of treating the scientific account as if it were itself metaphysical or religious; it challenges the tendency to make a religion of science —or a science of religion—a dogmatic act which destroys the moral dynamic of man. Indeed, many men of science are confronted with unexpected implications of their own thought and are beginning to accept, for instance, the trans-spatial and trans-temporal nature of matter itself.

RELIGIOUS PERSPECTIVES attempts to show the fallacy of the

apparent irrelevance of God in history. The Series submits that no convincing image of man can arise, in spite of the many ways in which human thought has tried to reach it, without a philosophy of human nature and human freedom which does not exclude God. This image of *Homo cum Deo* implies the highest conceivable freedom, the freedom to step into the very fabric of the universe, a new formula for man's collaboration with the creative process and the only one which is able to protect man from the terror of existence. This image implies further that the mind and conscience are capable of making genuine discriminations and thereby may reconcile the serious tensions between the secular and religious, the profane and sacred. The idea of the sacred lies in what it *is,* timeless existence. By emphasizing timeless existence against reason as a reality, we are liberated, in our communion with the eternal, from the otherwise unbreakable rule of "before and after." Then we are able to admit that all forms, all symbols in religions, by their negation of error and their affirmation of the actuality of truth, make it possible to experience that *knowing* which is above knowledge, and that dynamic passage of the universe to unending unity.

The volumes in this Series seek to challenge the crisis which separates, the crisis born out of a rationalism that has left no spiritual heirs, to make reasonable a religion that binds and to present the numinous reality within the experience of man. Insofar as the Series succeeds in this quest, it will direct mankind toward a reality that is eternal and away from a preoccupation with that which is illusory and ephemeral.

For man is now confronted with his burden and his greatness: "He calleth to me, Watchman, what of the night? Watchman, what of the night?"[1] Perhaps the anguish in the human soul may be assuaged by the answer, by the *assimilation* of the person in God: "The morning cometh, and also the night: if ye will inquire, inquire ye: return, come."[2]

RUTH NANDA ANSHEN

New York, 1961

[1] Isaiah 21:11.
[2] Isaiah 21:12.

Preface

THIS IS AN ESSAY IN THE OBVIOUS. THE MORE obvious its sentences seem, the better pleased will their author be. For philosophy has become so remote from experience and its branches so highly specialized, that it has little if anything to say to the thoughtful man who has not been initiated into the technical secrets of the craft. To be invited to contribute an essay to *Religious Perspectives* was an opportunity to revert to a manner of philosophizing which had proved fruitful in the past and might again prove fruitful. What I have tried to do is to examine the nature of thinking in its most general form, to accept man as an historical animal, and to claim no more for my conclusions than a certain probability.

It should be admitted at the outset that this essay is highly skeptical of the claims of logicians and scientists. It is more sympathetic to the nonrational modes of thinking than is usual. It emphasizes the aesthetic and religious aspects of systematic thought and it is willing to accept evidence from psychology and anthropology about the human mind. At the same time it does not deny the efficacy of rational thought nor its desirability, though it urges philosophers to recognize the disagreeable fact that even mathematics finds its premises and perhaps its structure too by means which are not ordinarily called logical.

It is addressed to the man who can take a few things for granted, especially the common sense of his adversaries, to the man who can read a book for what is in it, not for what is missing, to the man who does not need a footnote to justify—

15

as if one could—every statement of fact which is expressed, to the man in short who enjoys speculation. The moment sooner or later comes when a philosopher simply feels the need of saying what he has on his mind without always searching for someone who has said it before him. That moment came to me when I was invited to write this essay and for that I am especially grateful. In the past my books have been written in libraries; this has been written in the country and at the seashore. Its lack of references to authorities may be explained by that fact. And if that is a weakness, we can say that this is a work of the speculative imagination and dismiss it as that.

GEORGE BOAS

Baldwin, Maryland
Cotuit, Massachusetts

1
Reason and Experience

I SHALL BEGIN THIS EXAMINATION OF THE limits of reason by making a distinction between two kinds of sentences, the historical and the eternal. Any simple statement of fact, such as, "It is raining," or, "The snowdrops are in bloom," or, "I can't find my rubbers," I shall call an historical sentence. It is historical in the sense that it is true only of a dated and localized event. In the instances given the date is the present and the place "the here." But the tense and locality are indifferent to the nature of the sentence. Thus in my usage a sentence may be historical even if it is a prophecy.

In contrast to such sentences there are some which are true, or which may be true, regardless of date and place. Universal laws, generalizations, and mathematical formulas are quite different from historical statements and I shall call them eternal. "Rain falls on the just and the unjust alike"; "Snowdrops are the first flowers to bloom in the spring"; "Men who are absorbed in philosophical writing misplace their personal possessions"—these are examples of eternal statements, even though they may not be true. The people who make them think that they are true and, what is more, they think that they are always and everywhere true. They are eternal in the sense of being timeless, not in the sense of being immortal or ever-lasting.

In this essay I am more interested in historical statements than in eternal statements, though of course their interrelations are of the greatest importance. Furthermore, the sphere of reason is confined to the eternal, and the historical is only tangential to it.

Any historical sentence will be found upon reflection to be based upon the following conditions which are psychological, though the psychological conditions in questions are determined by social causes and not entirely by the isolated dreaming of the individual who pronounces them. This, I hope, will become clearer as we progress.

1. *The question to which it is the answer.*

Why should a man look up from his work and say, "It is raining"? Assuming that I am the man who says it, as my eye wanders about my study I find dozens of things which I might have said, things about my books, the plants which are growing on my window sills, the birds which are chirping in the bushes just outside, the magnifying glass on my desk, the Latin dictionary which is on the floor beside me instead of being in its place in the bookcase, the scarlet package of cigarettes which is lying on the green blotter next to the bottle of black ink, and the half-dozen pencils which stick up like bristles in an old medicine jar in the corner next to the lamp. If I make no comment on these things but do notice that it is raining, it is because I did not expect it to rain since it was sunny this morning when I began to work. Now I do not pretend that I said to myself, "What is the weather like?" and thereupon looked out of the window to see. But it was this unusual and unanticipated sight which caught my attention. Had I said to someone, "It is raining," and had that person already noticed it, and had he been in an uncharitable mood, he might well have replied sarcastically, "What did you think it was doing?" Or if I had awakened this morning to find it raining, I should probably not comment on it now. For no matter how intense our love for the obvious, we seldom go through a day repeating the same observations with which we wake up.

The psychological factors which determine what sentences we shall express are of course various. They may be frequently the observation, as just exemplified, that things are not as we expected them to be. But they may be questions put to us by other people, either our associates, or the authors of books, or just simple puzzles which we are trying to solve. They may arise out of our practical life, as when we want to look up a word in the Latin dictionary, look for the volume on the shelf where it belongs, do not find it, look round the room, and then see it on the floor. Or we want to put on our rubbers, look for them in their usual place, do not find them, and finally say, "I can't find my rubbers." Such a sentence may be a concealed appeal for help, rather than a declarative sentence, or even a criticism of hidden enemies who purposely misplace one's possessions in order to be troublesome. Then there are sentences which emerge out of what is wrongly called idle curiosity, wrongly because curiosity is never completely idle but only seems so to those who do not recognize its goal.

Behind the questioning about what is happening, where things are, or what has taken place, lies the philosophical assumption that the natural order ought not to change but should exhibit a constant and predictable pattern. This pattern or order is usually expressed in eternal sentences or scientific laws. Consequently any descriptive assertion of fact can be interpreted as emerging out of the observation that some eternal statement has been violated. Whatever changes occur, we imagine, must occur in a regular manner, and if we fail to see the regularity, we ask a question. If we were convinced that it would rain every morning from ten o'clock until noon, there would be little occasion for saying at ten o'clock, "It is raining." If our conviction were strong and we looked up at ten o'clock and found that it was not raining, then we should ask why and say, "Why, the sun is shining!" as if this were an unnatural and unpredictable event. This philosophical assumption of the regularity of nature, of the possibility of always discovering some unity beneath or behind or above the apparent diversity, is the source of all science. But it will be observed that whatever unity is found is always found following one of the prepositions in question. It cannot be expressed in literal terms and the words "beneath," "behind," and "above" are all metaphorical. The unity is what we are looking for; the diversity is what we encounter. In short, experience is the origin of science and philosophy only in the sense that it gives rise to our questions. It becomes the terminus of knowledge when it answers them.

The sentences which we have used are historical, not eternal, sentences. Logic has nothing to do with history.[1] There may, for instance, be some general principle defining the whereabouts of rubbers and Latin dictionaries, but once such subjects have been elevated to the realm of eternity, they have ceased to be things and have been purified into concepts. This is accomplished by the scientist's power of abstraction. When Galileo spoke of falling bodies, to take but one example, he was not talking about this or that falling body made of wood, stone, or paper falling in air or through water. He must have known that such bodies do not obey the Law of Falling Bodies at all, for he could not deny that bits of paper fall more slowly through the air than stones do. But he wanted a conceptual situation such that an eternal statement could be framed and he got one by disregarding the material out of which the bodies were made and the medium through which they fell. He had no prior information to tell him that the medium would make any difference; his genius enabled him to imagine a situation in which all the variations in fall would be eliminated. And, as we all know, he was successful in framing a law descriptive of such a situation. Now that the law is established, it is accepted as if it were obvious. It gives us a rule by which we can determine whether things are as they ought to be. It defines the diversity

---

[1] Cf. Clerk Maxwell as quoted by Charles P. Curtis, Jr. and Ferris Greenslet in their *The Practical Cogitator*, rev. ed. (Boston: Houghton Mifflin, 1953), pp. 244 f. "It is a metaphysical doctrine that from the same antecedents follow the same consequents. No one can gainsay this. But it is not of much use in a world like this, in which the same antecedents never again concur, and nothing ever happens twice. Indeed, for aught we know, one of the antecedents might be the precise date and place of the event, in which case experience would go for nothing."

of events as deviations from the norm, for it is the norm. When we see feathers fluttering down through the air, we no longer ask why they do not drop like stones. But if they fluttered down in a vacuum instead of dropping, we would ask a question about it.

The expectation that events should occur in a constant fashion is justified by science, but not by experience, unless experience is already guided by science. If we identify Nature with everyday Nature, the things which we see about us in time and space, Nature is far from uniform. But if we identify it with what science tells us about things and events, then it is indeed uniform for one cannot have eternal statements which are variable. Even when such statements concern the course of events and thus seem to be historical, they express that sequence in timeless symbols. Thus in the Temperate Zone we can say that there are four seasons; but the actual length of each season may vary from year to year, as when we speak of early springs, late winters, precocious autumns, and prolonged summers. This is nonsensical if we are talking of the astronomical seasons. The scientific winter begins on December 21 and ends on March 20, though the weather may be unusually warm at the beginning and unusually cold at the end. The equinoxes and solstices mark the beginnings and ends of the seasons for the scientific mind; for the flesh-and-blood human being, they are determined by the weather. If we are surprised to find that history, as distinguished from science, is not invariable, that is because we have had it drummed into our heads from childhood that scientific truth is the standard to which history ought to conform. We are delighted when it does and raise questions when it does not. But we might well raise the question of how science succeeds in organizing the chaos of history into an orderly design.

2. *The general terms to which we are habituated.*

All things and events have names, though we may not always know them. When something radically new is discovered or invented, it is given a name at once. This is done so that people can talk about it. These names are either the symbols of classes, or names like John Jones or The French Revolution or This Book, which belong only to certain specifiable individuals. Class-names are what are usually called common nouns. The names of individual things and events are proper nouns. "Rubbers" is a common noun; "My rubbers" is a proper noun. We learn this distinction in the first grades in school, but we do not learn its consequences.

Any thing or event is likely to belong to a great variety of classes. Hence the common noun which will be used to identify it may vary according to the linguistic habits of the user. My Latin dictionary is "Harper's Latin Dictionary, founded on the translation of Freund's Latin-German Lexicon, edited by E. A. Andrews, revised, enlarged, and in great part rewritten by Charlton T. Lewis and Charles Short." It is possible that some pedant citing one of its definitions would refer to it in that way, followed by place and date of publication. But it is also just a member of the class, Latin dictionaries, of the larger class of dictionaries of all languages, of books, of things made of paper and hence of carbon compounds, of combustible objects, of objects on which children can be seated at table when the chairs are too low for them, of things in which, unfortunately, ferns can be pressed, of almost prismatic shapes, of essential adjuncts to scholarship, of material objects weighing something like eight pounds, and in fact of other classes as well. Which of these common nouns am I going to use in referring to it? This depends entirely on what I want to do with it. If I want to compare its definitions with those of some other Latin dictionary, it would be Harper's. But if I simply wanted to look up the meaning of some Latin word, it would be only a Latin dictionary. When I put it in my armchair to prevent my cocker spaniel from jumping upon the chair, going to sleep there, and leaving the pillow covered with hairs, its place could as well be taken by Liddell and Scott or any other large bit of uncomfortable matter. The children who pressed ferns in it cared little for its lexicographical information and those who have sat on it at table cared less.

I am not suffering from the illusion that when Freund wrote his lexicon he intended it to be put to all these uses. Hence a person could sneer at what seems like my magisterial pedantry and say that "really" it is a Latin dictionary and that's all it is. But "really" in this context means no more than what the original author of the thing intended it to be. God intended Adam to dress and keep the Garden of Eden and not to eat of the Tree of Knowledge. But Adam did not dress and keep it and he did eat of the Tree of Knowledge. But this is standard operating procedure. Historical objects have a way of not being what they "really" are, if we mean by "really" what their makers intended them to be. It could, I imagine, be plausibly argued that eggs were not intended to be fried but to be hatched, that trees were not intended to be burned in fireplaces but to produce other trees, that water was intended to be drunk and not to flood cities. In fact, much moralizing has been wasted in pointing out the original intentions of God and Nature and how they have been perverted.

Though we all recognize the futility of such arguments, we need class-names to clarify experiences for ourselves and to communicate them to others. Hence we have set up various contexts in which the appropriate classes are defined. One of the most interesting traits of the human mind is its ability to grasp the contexts of ambiguous words which are not to be confused. A plant may be either a form of vegetation or a factory; in American slang to be fired means to be discharged from one's job, but it also means to be excited with enthusiasm for something. How do we know the context? Only by accumulated experience. It is conceivable that a foreigner hearing that someone was "down at the plant," might think the person to be engaged in horticulture. We cannot discuss here how words slither from one context to another and shift their meanings as they go, but that this occurs is known to everyone.

What is of more importance is that the attempt to fix the meanings of words as of the date of their origin is always vain.

For though each science inevitably classifies things according to a context which it has determined, we men in everyday life classify them according to our historically determined interests. The context of a science is equivalent to the questions which the science asks. If physics is defined as the science of matter in motion, as it still is in small dictionaries, then anything which cannot be derived from matter in motion will be irrelevant to physics. Motion and rest, velocity, acceleration, deceleration, mass and weight, and directions will be relevant; but color, taste, sound, smell, and textures will be irrelevant except to the extent that they can be correlated with moving objects.

Actually no science has remained where it was at its origin. The shifts in human interest have produced shifts in scientific questions. And the old dogmas are abandoned or corrected as the new questions are answered. The question of whether the isotopes of a given element are "really" that element or not makes sense only if we differentiate the elements exclusively on the principle of their atomic weights and assume that each element will have only one atomic weight. Again, the question of whether an organism is a plant or an animal will be raised only if we first decide that the two classes are mutually exclusive and that, let us say, one class absorbs oxygen and combines it with carbon to form carbon dioxide and the other absorbs carbon dioxide and liberates the oxygen from it, returning it to the air. When the time came to organize the plants in some systematic way, we find Caesalpinus classifying them according to their fruit, Ray on whether they produced flowers or not, Morison on whether they were woody or herbaceous, and Linnaeus on their sexual organs. The question of which is the natural or correct or real way of classifying them turns out to be artificial. For if we think of the sciences as what living beings have thought about things, and not as a body of eternal statements generated by logic alone, then there is no fundamental difference between the common nouns, the classifiers, used by scientists and those used by the rest of us.

Behind all classification lies the assumption that if something belongs to one class in a given context, then it cannot also belong to another in that context. Classes must not overlap. But the class to which we assign a thing is determined by the context in which we are thinking about it, not by the thing itself cut off from all human interests. Hence though I may use a chemical term when speaking of my rubbers, I am not thinking of them as chemical substances when I do so. The noun is used by me because it has become customary in America to use it in this connection; if I had been educated in England, I might call them gum-boots. I have never heard of anyone referring to his rubbers as water-proof shoe covers.

All that we demand of a common noun is that others will grasp its meaning. But the fact that we do use common nouns suggests that we habitually think of a thing as properly belonging more to one class than to another to which it might be assigned. That class provides a "correct" name which indicates the "real" nature of its members. The utility of all this is not to be depreciated. For once something is classified, then it ought to be possible to determine some of its properties from what you know of other members of the class. Once you learn as a child that a whale is not a fish but a mammal, you go on to deduce that it must suckle its young, probably be viviparous, and breathe through lungs instead of gills. You do not observe all this for yourself; you observe a whale swimming and spouting. Its mammalian nature is learned, usually from others, and then employed to furnish new information about the creature. And by the principle of generic cloisters, we also learn that if the thing is a mammal and not a fish, it will not lay eggs like fishes. Whereupon we stumble over the platypus. The platypus does not seem to have studied the principles of classification; it is a traitor to its real nature if its real nature is mammalian. Its existence may horrify the classifiers but that is because they have accepted too uncritically the existence of classes. Science gives us a context ready-made; it has become customary to classify the ordinary things about us according to this context. Even if we say that a thing is really what it is in scientific discourse, we should also keep in mind that it is just as really a number of other things.

If we keep cool, no harm is done by the custom of calling a thing's real nature the nature described by some science or other. But unfortunately the use of the adverb "really" has induced us to make a distinction between what a thing really is and what it appears to be. That distinction arises on the level of common sense when we say that a man looks like his brother, or appears to be honest but is really a liar, "is not himself" when under the influence of alcohol. In all such cases we have a rule for determining what a person is really: he is what he usually is. But note that we assume once more that a person, like everything else, has a constant and invariable nature which is not always observed. This assumption cannot be verified under ordinary conditions and that is why we have to use such figurative language as the prepositions "underneath," "behind," "above," or "within." "Underneath his frivolous exterior lay a bleeding heart"; "Behind his gloomy countenance was a spirit of happiness"; "Above his momentary divagations he marched steadily forward"; "Externally he was miserly and avaricious, but within he was liberal and generous." (I assume no responsibilities for the mixed metaphors.)

We seldom ask ourselves why human beings should not be miserly in some situations and generous in others, gloomy at some times and cheerful at others, frivolous in the presence of others and serious when alone. We take it for granted that a person ought to be one thing or the other and, if we actually find that he refuses to be what he ought to be, we then decide either that he is a psychological monster who lacks character or that he is really one thing and only appears to be the other.

The reason why scientists can reveal the underlying nature of things is that they have a technique for setting up systems of tests to which the things in question will respond always or on the whole in the same way. The circumstances under which they behave in some other way are irrelevant to the kind of question which the scientist is putting to them. An anatomist does not have to know whether the cadaver which he is dissecting was a charming companion, a lover of books, stupid or intelligent, monogamous or polygamous, a Christian or an atheist, or whether he had a preference for Bourbon whiskey. Similarly a chemist when he is asking chemical questions does not care whether silver is used for tableware or money, whether hydrochloric acid is found in the human stomach, whether hydrogen peroxide bleaches the hair. But on the level of common sense all such things are of interest and at times of greater interest than what science has to say.

Therefore it would be misleading to say that silver is "really" a metal with the atomic weight of 107.88 and the atomic number 47 and only appears to be quarters and dimes and forks and spoons. That some metals look like silver and are not silver is of course true. But such errors in identification should give rise to no metaphysical questions about appearance and reality. There is no reason why anything should be a specimen of any particular class rather than of any other, except the reason of verbal usage. But since we are all forced to conform to verbal usage, we shall often fall victim to its implied metaphysics, the metaphysics of enduring inner natures.

3. *The univalence of words.*

The rejection of change and the metaphysics of enduring natures are accompanied by the assumption that words must always mean the same thing. This is usually expressed as the Law of Identity. It simply means that a given term must retain its meaning throughout an argument. If this were not observed, it is clear that one could never be sure that the conclusion of a syllogism referred to the same thing as the premises. Jevons in his classic textbook of Aristotelian logic, *Elementary Lessons in Logic,* a text in which many generations learned the rules of formal reasoning, gives the following example of a fallacy derived from the violation of this law.

All criminal actions ought to be punished by law;
Prosecutions for theft are criminal actions;
Therefore prosecutions for theft ought to be punished by law.

It is doubtful whether anyone, even if he had not studied logic, would fail to detect the ambiguity in the term "criminal actions," or that he would deny the desirability of preserving a stable meaning in the terms which express his argument. The rule would apply whether one was arguing in syllogisms or in any other form of reasoning.

Nevertheless, words do change their meaning to some extent in the various contexts in which they occur, but the change is always historical. We have to name things either by words which we have inherited or which we have invented; there is nothing else that we can do. The problem of applying an old term to a new situation can be solved only by solving the delicate problem which always arises of how much similarity is equivalent to identity and how little determines difference. In technical exercises, such as we come upon in mathematics or the sciences, we can invent terms; the technical names for chemical compounds, plants, animals, diseases, and geometrical figures will do as an example. But in ordinary discourse we are more likely to use traditional speech. Traditional speech, insofar as its vocabulary is concerned, can do nothing to make precise those shades of meaning which vary with different contexts.

This is most dramatically illustrated in courts of law where certain terms are as carefully defined as human beings can make them and where it has to be decided whether a certain act is an example of the class of acts named by the term in question. A man, let us say, is charged with murder. Murder obviously is a form of homicide. But one can kill another man deliberately, in cold blood, with forethought, or one can kill another man accidentally. One can kill a man in the heat of passion or in a fit of madness or in self-defense or to avenge an act for which the state has not punished him and for which one firmly believes he should be punished. In the good old days it was not so serious to kill a slave or a serf as to kill a freeman, to kill a commoner as to kill a nobleman. Since those times various degrees of homicide have been distinguished so that a man who accidentally kills another is not considered to be presumptively guilty of the same crime as a man is who kills another deliberately. Anyone who has ever sat on a court-martial will recall how carefully the manual states the criteria of the different crimes and misdemeanors. In nonmilitary courts one proceeds on the basis of precedent. But in both cases it will be discovered that the history of legal terminology has moved in the direction of finer distinctions, for it has been seen that the psychological condition of the accused, the circumstances surrounding the act, the motivation, all have a bearing upon the nature of what has been done. In spite of the sixth commandment, the great majority of clergymen have agreed that killing enemies, certain criminals, and at times heretics, is not unjustifiable homicide.

But such a development in the meanings of terms will be found wherever we have to name things and events intimately connected with human life. Novels often dwell upon psychological differences to such an extent that one comes to believe that such verbs as "to love" and "to hate" have become so vague as to have lost their utility. We are interested in a man's sincerity, in his motives, in the object of his affection and hatred, in the causes of his emotions, and we have the feeling that these all particularize it. We no longer feel able to lop off a simple act from its antecedents and consequents and call it by a simple name. Yet when we wish to talk about it, the best we can do is to give it a blanket label. The problem turns into a metaphysical one. It is the problem of objective frontiers, of how far an object or event extends. In the case of murder in any degree, there is a common element: homicide. In the case of love there is an emotion. As long as we think of nothing but such common elements, the traditional terms will do. And perhaps if we were not so much bent on praising and blaming others for what they do, the traditional terms would never have to be changed. But when we come to believe that enduring love is more praiseworthy than momentary love, then we also come to believe that the two should be distinguished verbally. And when we come to believe that to kill a man in battle is not so blameworthy as to kill him in times of peace, we again look for two names with which to ticket the same act.

A similar process can be observed in the history of scientific names. In biology it has been desirable to group plants and animals together not only for descriptive purposes but also, since the rise of evolutionism, for explanatory. As late as Linnaeus it was assumed that only minor variations would be found within a species and that between species there would be no intermediate forms. But during the nineteenth and twentieth centuries, when certain individuals and groups of individuals were studied more closely, it was found that frequently it was merely a matter of convention where one would cut off the various species of a genus from one another. A single species, such as Darwin's finches on the Galápagos Islands, was discovered to have established different subspecies which would not interbreed or at least would not produce offspring if they did. A. J. Cain in his *Animal Species and Their Evolution* points out that the great tit is a bird which ranges from the British Isles to Japan and from Central Siberia into Indonesia. It has developed at least four large groups with marked morphological differences. One can cut off the extremes of this collection of birds easily enough, but in between there are forms which are very similar. In fact, it has been said simply that a species is a species if a competent systematist says it is.[2] Class-names have been assigned on the basis of morphological similarities, on the willingness or ability of individuals to interbreed, on intersterility, and on unity of phylogenetic origin. Each method serves a special purpose. Now that isotopes have been found for numerous elements, one wonders whether some physical chemist will not suggest that

[2] Cain, *op. cit.,* p. 51.

an element is the name for a group of substances having "more or less" the same atomic weight.

Be that as it may, one thing is certain: the observed similarities which are the basis for grouping things together must seem important to us for intellectual or practical reasons. If we are not painters, we shall use the names of colors superficially and not bother about distinctions which a trained eye will see. Any green from a yellow-green to a blue-green will be green and any red from an orange-red to a red-violet will be red. If we are not students of literature, we shall not hesitate to call any poem of fourteen lines a sonnet, regardless of its rhyme-scheme, and shall not distinguish between Shakespearean sonnets, Miltonian sonnets, Keatsian sonnets, and Merrill-Moorean sonnets. If we are not musicologists, we shall use a term like "sonata" without differentiating between the sonatas of Alessandro Scarlatti, Mozart, and Brahms. And if we are deeply serious and interested in the peculiarities of whatever object or event is before us, we shall throw up our hands in despair and conclude that everything is simply itself and let it go at that.

This does not deny that real and important similarities can be found. But it does deny that the detection of similarities is the most important thing that can be done when we are trying to understand the world about us. General terms like general laws are useful, uniquely useful, for simplifying nature. But they do not tell us all that we want or need to know. To see the importance of distinctions in life as distinguished from science, we have only to study a book on moral casuistry, if reading a book is needed. We might think that our experience in trying to understand ourselves and those close to us would suffice to show us that no two moral situations are precisely the same. One examines one's conscience and asks, "Have I lied?" or, "Have I been cowardly?" or, "Have I been disloyal?" These are not questions which can be answered by looking into a book. There is no necessity here of going into all the details which determine a person's acts: his motives, his foresight of the consequences, his regard for the person toward whom he is acting or who might be affected by the act, his general state of mind at the moment of acting—he is bewildered, calm, "not himself," swept away by mob hysteria, under strong parental, social, or economic pressure, misled by false information. Yet all such details, we feel, have to be taken into account in determining precisely what he has done. Just as in the case of homicide we do not say that the man who has killed another accidentally has done the same thing as the man who kills another deliberately, though in both cases a man has been killed, so the man who lies to his wife who is dying of cancer and lies to her out of pity, is not doing the same thing as the man who lies under oath on the witness stand. Yet a lie has been told in both cases. Books in ethics have to set up certain classes of acts and, if such books are necessary—which is of course questionable—their necessity arises out of our desire to understand the acts of human beings.

Unfortunately class-names carry with them a connotation of value. It is assumed that the definition of a class, or of a common noun, sets up a standard of membership in the class defined, which is obvious; but it is also assumed that the things to which we give a class-name have some obligation to live up to the standard we have imposed upon them, which is far from obvious. When we come upon natural objects which do not conform to our definitions of the class to which we have assigned them—Siamese twins, two-headed calves, albinos, dwarfs and giants—we call them by disagreeable names: monsters, anomalies, abnormalities, sports. But in some quarters it is assumed that works of art too should fall into definable classes and that it is the duty of the artist to make his productions conform to the definitions provided by aestheticians and critics. Once a definition of a sonnet has been established, for instance, the critic seems to feel that it is obligatory for poets to write verses which closely approximate what the definition demands. The late Merrill Moore, to whom we referred above, wrote several hundred short poems which he called sonnets.

Critics have been known to object to them on the ground that they are not "true" sonnets. But true sonnets are simply those which have been selected by the critics in question on the ground that they have common characteristics. These characteristics are obviously what is left over when the individual traits of the various poems have been subtracted from them.

Why should these characteristics be more important than the individual traits? Among sonnets we have several subclasses, of which two are Shakespearean and Miltonic. Each subclass again has common traits, rhyme-scheme and fourteen lines being the most obvious. But it requires no study to see that no two Shakespearean sonnets are exactly alike; if they were, what would be the sense of reading more than one of them? Nor is the formal structure of them the most interesting thing about them. If it were, one could symbolize the metric scheme by dots and dashes, omitting the words, and the rhyme-scheme by A's and B's, beat out the former on a drum and pronounce the latter, and think that one was reading the sonnet. On that hypothesis any woman will do to marry and any god to worship. There is no self-evident reason why the general is more inherently valuable than the particular, the formal than the material, in spite of tradition to the contrary. What looks like a reason is simply our confusion of the rationally intelligible and the good. But that good is a purely intellectual good, a good in science and pseudo-science.

4. *Atomism.*

By "atomism" I mean the intellectual technique of dividing a subject matter into items which are self-enclosed, cut off from one another, and related to one another externally. Such items are considered as things (*res*) rather than as processes. Whatever their relations, they retain their internal identity. They become units which can be added together to make collections which in turn may, and in some respects always will, have characteristics which are different from their own. The atomistic technique in science is first recorded in the fragments of Leucippus and Democritus. Judging from the badly shattered remains of their thoughts, their aim was to explain everything as spatial configurations of the smallest possible bits of matter moving about in empty space. Each atom had a shape of its own and was in motion, but otherwise all atoms were alike. All the sensory properties of the world, the colors, sounds, and so on, were, as far as we know, to be explained as effects produced in us by the various atomic configurations.

It is no longer possible to discover how this idea arose, but we can see how it fits in with ordinary uncritical experience of the tactual and visual world. The things which we handle are indeed cut off from one another and move about or can be moved about with no apparent internal change. Marbles and billiard balls are the stock examples of this. No one who is not a physicist thinks that a marble rolling across the floor changes in any way other than in its position in space. And position does not seem to be an inherent trait of material objects. Moreover, insofar as objects are visual, their frontiers are fairly clear and we can tell where each thing is by looking. It is true that visually things do change their size as they recede into the distance. But close at hand we see where a physical object begins and ends. Billiard balls, like sticks and stones, do not appear to melt into one another. They are clear-cut, have definite silhouettes, and if we are in any doubt about their limits, we can touch them and settle our doubts.

But the atomistic technique is used to form our conception of everything which we name. Nothing could be less tangible and visible than a human being. His body may be thought of as a material object bounded in space and cut out of its surroundings. But his personality is about as fluid a being as any being can be. To begin with, it is in a constant state of change as new experiences enter into it, flow out of it to affect other human beings, and conflict or harmonize with one another. It possesses something called memory through which the past is not left behind like a spatial area through which the person has moved, but is retained. But it does not retain all the past nor is what it retains always present to consciousness. On the contrary, past things come and go in an unpredictable manner, going when we want to retain them, being retained when we would prefer their absence. Moreover, a person forms patterns of behavior called habits which no inanimate object seems to form, patterns which become compulsive, which after being learned drop out of consciousness and seem to be automatic, which require less time to perform as they are repeated until they appear to be almost instantaneous.

Though it has been customary to refer to perceptual experiences as impressions made upon the mind by objects in a world usually called external, we now know that such experiences are not only selected by the person having them because of his interests, anticipations, and repulsions, but actually modified by him in various ways. A person who hates something may judge its size to be bigger than it would be if measured, let us say, by a pair of calipers. We often see what we are looking for, hear what we are listening for, find what we are searching for, though thousands of other possible perceptions could be experienced. Each of our verbs which refers to a perceptual experience is tied to another which indicates an active pursuit of the experience in question. We have mentioned seeing and looking, hearing and listening, in which cases the verbs are given two different names; but we also taste "to see" what something tastes like and can also simply have the experience of a flavor. To feel, to touch, to smell, are, as everyone knows, also used both in the sense of doing something and of having something happen to one. If one sniffs something to see what it smells like, one is not simply inertly waiting for something to happen; an odor does not merely drift in and out of one's consciousness. And if one does not sniff it, one may not smell it at all. The traditional variations in sensory percepts need not be dwelt upon since they are known to all: variations attributed to the age, health, and normal perspicacity of the person involved. Hence to reconstruct a world out of sensory perceptions would be about as scientifically useful as reconstructing one out of dreams.

In spite of the fluidity and mutability and indefiniteness of our personalities, our use of the personal pronouns seems to warrant our considering them as hard cores which retain their identity throughout time. We refer to what *we* did some years ago as if the *we* recalling the past were actually present in the past. We project ourselves similarly into the future though we know that we shall have changed when the future becomes the present. Furthermore, unless the statute of limitations is applied, we can be held responsible for things done in the more or less remote past and are occasionally rewarded for having done them. Ironically enough, there is sufficient awareness of personal transitoriness to make reformers urge us to hitch our wagons to stars, to develop consistency of character, to be true to ourselves, and in short to do everything we can to defeat the passage of time. Nothing better illustrates the discrepancy between thought and experience than this. If personality were as fixed as our personal pronouns would make us believe, there would be no need for such programs of reform. It would be absurd to tell a man of permanent character to be permanent. Our notion of the hard core of personality is again evidence of our custom of transferring our notion of visual and tactual objects, material things, to a world where they cannot be found.

The tactual and visual basis for our atomism can also be recognized when we stop to think of what other kinds of world might be imagined. Dogs, as we know, are more accustomed to a world of odors than to one of sights. Now no dog, nor any other animal as far as I know, is purely olfactory. But one can imagine what an olfactory world would be like. First, "things" would have no sharply defined contours, for odors do not have shapes. Second, they would be evanescent rather than permanent, for at least the odors of which we human beings are aware come and go as we become habituated to them. Third, their spatial location would be indefinite: we might have a vague idea of where such an object might be, but it would float about and the best we could do would be to locate it at the point of its greatest intensity. Analogous remarks could be made about objects which would be purely or simply sonorous or even gustatory, though we could not have any tastes unless we were able to put the objects into our mouths (which would mean giving them tactual qualities) or licking them (which would require finding them first). The absurdity of such a picture of experience is enough to show how interconnected our senses are and how abstract, in the literal meaning of that word, our visual and tactual universe is.

Yet one cannot deny the real existence of odors, tastes, and sounds. They are there just as shapes and weights and velocities are there. But they are hard to accommodate to a purely visual and tactual interpretation of the world and since human beings seldom rely on them for information, we neglect them. But what is more troubling is our attempt to treat them as if they too were "things" located in external space in the same way that material objects are. It cannot be denied that physical science has given us extraordinarily successful explanations of the origin of such experiences on an atomistic basis, but it has been done at the cost of robbing them of precisely that which makes them experiences. Such explanations succeed by a radical simplification of what we do in life. To take but one example, that of sound, no one would seriously dispute the theory that sounds arise from the impact of air waves—usually —upon our auditory end organs. It is a beautiful demonstration which can be corroborated by simple and easily controlled experiments. But neither would anyone assert that an air wave by itself is a sound. And it is the sounds which we hear, not the air waves. The manipulation of air waves by drawing a bow across a string or hitting a metal sheet or blowing through a tube will produce sounds to be sure, but, as every child soon learns in school, that is only one half of the story. The other half lies in the auditory apparatus of the sentient human being.

When we come to processes, events, biographies, and histories, the turning of them into things is downright misleading, though our verbal customs force us into doing this. When, for instance, we speak of a war, we think of it as cut off at its beginning and end and also as having lateral edges. If we are going to write history, there is nothing else that we can do. But nevertheless any historian will testify that the notion of events having a beginning in the sense that a yardstick or a brick has a beginning is nonsensical. Historical events are the intertwining of long strands which go well back into the remote past and which will go on into the remote future. Is the history of the United States a part of English history? If so, why is it not also a part of French, Dutch, and Spanish history? If not, does it begin on July 4, 1776, or with the ratification of the Constitution? Is the Revolution a war between the colonies and Great Britain or an incident in the Wars between France and Great Britain? Such questions can be answered only by fiat, which in the long run is what tradition induces a man to queston. We know that events are all intertwined, but in spite of this we try to untangle them, much as an anatomist dissects a muscle out of the bundle of muscles of which it is a part. Otherwise they could not be handled. Our technique of thinking in terms of things forces us to do this.

5. *Methodological rules.*

Besides the rules of logic and verbal custom there are certain methodological rules which have been set up over the centuries to guide and control rational investigations. These rules are not so stringent as the laws of logic, and it has been seen, as the years have gone by, that they may be abrogated. Yet we need some rules if we are not to lapse into caprice or daydreaming. I shall indicate a few such principles simply to illustrate what I am talking about.

(a) Nothing can come from nothing (*ex nihilo nihil*).

(b) Nature does nothing in vain.

(c) There is no action at a distance.

(d) Nature always follows the simplest course.

(e) The same causes always produce the same effects.

(f) That which has a beginning must have an end.

(g) Things tend to persist in their own natures.

(h) Ultimate laws are mechanical.[3]

Now there is not a single one of these sentences whose truth cannot be questioned nor one which has not been questioned. If they are taken as descriptions, they go well beyond the experience of any one individual or of any group of individuals. The fact that some of them are in conflict with others is pretty good proof that they are neither innate ideas nor self-evident. As a matter of fact, it is wiser to interpret them as rules of the game. They tell us what to avoid in the way of explanation. If, for instance, there were such a thing as creation *ex nihilo,* it would look as if the occurrence of created events would be inexplicable. Hence even those scientists who believed in the creation of the universe by God held that there was only one act of creation and that subsequent to it everything was caused by some other detectable thing. If there were such a thing as action at a distance, anything anywhere might be held to be the cause of anything else anywhere else. If Nature were not uniform, scientific laws might be true here and false there and falling bodies might fall faster in Europe than in America or have fallen more slowly in ancient times than they do now.

Without entering into a discussion of the various interpretations which have been given of these principles, I think it fair to say that they all have one purpose in view: to permit the investigator to establish generalizations which will vary neither from time to time, from place to place, from one social complex to another, nor from one individual scientist to another. If one should say that no two people ever do have exactly the same experiences, ever do observe things happening in the same way, ever do discover Nature's single purpose, that would be true but irrelevant. For these principles as rules serve the purpose of explaining away the obvious differences in personal

[3] E.g., Clerk Maxwell: "When a physical phenomenon can be completely described as a change in the configuration and motion of a material system, the dynamical explanation of that phenomenon is said to be complete." This is quoted along with several other opinions saying the same by J. B. Stallo, *The Concepts and Theories of Modern Physics* (New York: Appleton, 1884), p. 18.

experiences. We see something coming out of nothing each time we mix pigments on a palette to produce a color which was not in either of them. We see the purposelessness of Nature in the overproduction of sperms and eggs, to say nothing of individuals. We see action at a distance every time a person obeys a command. We see the complexity of Nature in the fantastic variety of species and subspecies of animals and plants. We see that the same causes do not always produce the same effects when we observe the effect of a drop in temperature on a group of human beings. We do not see things which begin coming to an end for the simple reason that we do not see the beginning of anything. As for the persistence of natures, everything which we know changes from moment to moment. And when we are told that only mechanical laws are satisfactory and complete explanations, we ask what mechanical law explains why a man trumps his partner's trick. It is because we see such things every day that the rules were invented.

For if rational discourse is a simplification and purification of what people see and do, science cannot be experience even when it is experimentation. The moment when a man passes from experience to generalization, from history to logic, from time to eternity, he has rejected experience in favor of something more perfect, more unified, and more intelligible than experience. And the moment he moves in the other direction, the most he can hope for is something which will approximate more or less what it ought to be. What it ought to be is what it would be if scientific laws were historical descriptions, or if experience were logic. Insofar as there is a gap between the two realms, reason is incapable of bridging it.

I have tried, then, to distinguish between two sorts of sentence, one which I have called historical or statements of fact, and the other eternal or logical and mathematical. The former are conditioned by psychological causes: the questions to which they are the answers, the general terms to which we are habituated, the univalence of words, the atomizing of experience, and certain methodological rules. I have attempted neither to justify our usual methods of thinking nor to criticize them. It has seemed sufficient to make a difference between rough-and-ready experience and the ritualized customs of the reason. The following chapters will try to clarify both my assumptions and my conclusions.

2
The World of Time

LOGIC, WE HAVE SAID, HAS NOTHING TO DO with history. In the world of logic nothing happens; things do not come into being and pass away; nothing grows; there is no hope, no disappointment, no courage, no cowardice, no love, no hate. It is a world of relations between frozen concepts whose beauty lies in their inevitable and immutable bonds. It is a pattern like an enormous network, the knots of which are universals, the connecting threads relations. The human mind can travel along the threads and stop at the knots, but within the network nothing moves.

Over against this world is the world in which we live and die. It is the world whose inhabitants are individual particular things and events. In the language of the schools it is the world of existence as contrasted with the world of essence. It is this world which is usually called the realm of experience. It is a temporal world, a world of change, a world whose design has to be discovered through research which is sometimes painful and frequently futile, a world of problems, not answers.

The metaphysical question which has to be raised at this point is whether we ever encounter universals in experience. Do we see redness or patches of red, circularity or circles, matter or material beings, humanity or men and women? This is a question which has preoccupied philosophers since the time of Plato and, for all we know, from an even earlier time. The difficulty of answering it appears when we realize that as soon

42

as a baby recognizes similarities, he is involved in it. We shall not attempt to solve it here for the attempt would lead only to one more restatement of a point of view which would convince no adversary. We shall say dogmatically that as far as this essay is concerned, the items of experience are always individuals, not universals, that universals are constructed out of these either by the process of abstraction or that of generalization or that of purification. The psychological problems bound together with the formation of general ideas we shall not discuss. It is enough for our purposes if it is admitted that we do have general ideas. We can grant that we should never have a concept of redness, or of color in general for that matter, if our eyes were not sensitive to the reflection of certain wave lengths. We can also grant that we should never have a concept of redness if we had not seen red things. But on the other hand, once a general idea has been precipitated out of experience, it can be extended well beyond experience. If a man has an idea of a three-sided plane figure, he can go on and imagine, or define, figures with any number of sides up to infinity. Moreover, he can go through this process in fields less well explored than that of mathematics. He can imagine two-headed men, three-headed men, and men whose heads do grow beneath their shoulders. And he does not have to have seen such monsters in order to draw pictures of them.

Furthermore, once an idea has been formed of any class of things or events, we can continue to purify it until it includes almost everything. Such purification consists of dropping out of the idea those traits which it does not share with similar ideas. In the case of our plane figures, we purge them of the number of their sides and come out with plane figures. In the case of our many-headed men, we drop out the number of heads and come out with men. Indeed some philosophers have even gone so far as to form the concept of *Being* itself, a concept which leaves nothing out, including the unreal as well as the real. This exercise may be called climbing the Tree of Porphyry.[1] Unfortu-

[1] Those readers who have forgotten Logic I may wish to be reminded

nately at the top of the Tree there is nothing in particular, for a universal predicate by its very nature cannot particularize. Yet the pathos of purity is such that men will sacrifice all experience in order to purge their minds of all difference, all change, all existence.

At the same time it will be observed that we always attempt to find exemplifications of our general ideas, either by direct observation or by experimental testing. We hear of some outlandish animal and insist on seeing a picture of it, as if a picture were a satisfactory substitute for the thing represented. In the physical sciences an hypothesis is framed but is not accepted until it is corroborated by experimentation. We cannot actually see the molecules in a substance, to say nothing of the atoms and whatever is in the nucleus of the atom, but we can construct a method which will give us circumstantial evidence of their existence. We cannot directly observe the past, the future, or very distant regions of space, but again we have more or less reliable means for finding out something about them as if they were actually before us. But it must be remembered that such devices are themselves constructed through reasoning. If, for instance, we did not believe in the constancy of causal laws, natural rhythms and cycles, the applicability of certain op-

---

that Porphyry, a third-century figure, elaborated a pattern of the logical universe which ran from the most general term which he could think of, *Being,* down to individuals. It may be represented as follows:

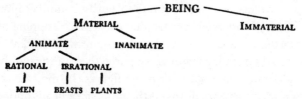

The classes are split up, as is clear, into mutually exclusive classes by what he thought of as a purely logical process. But he does not tell us why he chose the special differentiating traits which he used, i.e., why "material" instead of "moving," why "animate" instead of "terrestrial"? It is customary to add Plato, Socrates, and other individuals under *Men,* but there is no purely logical process by which any class can be proved to be exemplified.

erations in mathematics, we could not rely on the validity of experimental tests. The corroboration of reason through experience depends on rules laid down by the reason and yet no one believes in the conclusions of reasoning until they have been empirically demonstrated.

Experience not only is used in rational discourse to corroborate what logic tells us ought to exist, but also raises the questions which we try to answer. These questions manifestly may be of two sorts, *questions of fact* and *questions of policy*.

Questions of fact arise as soon as we perceive that things are not as they ought to be. We assume that they ought to be what they have been. And what they have been is what we remember them to have been or what the society of men interested in them have recorded them as being. We introduce here the premise that all events should exhibit a constant pattern, the pattern which is expounded in scientific laws. These laws establish a norm from which things of a given class ought not to deviate. If they do deviate from the established norm, we have either to correct the law or reclassify the things. Thus if a child is born with two heads, we may raise the question of why he is born with two heads; but if he is born with one head, we do not ask why he doesn't have two. But if enough children were bicephalic, we should have to set up two classes of human beings, the monocephalic and the bicephalic. The question would then be raised of the conditions under which a baby is born with only one head and of those under which he is born with two.

How many such cases are "enough"? There is no more a rule for settling this than there is for determining where one should cut off species from one another. As far as we know the normal child is monocephalic but that simply means that the overwhelming majority of babies have but one head. If once in a while we come upon a bicephalic child, it is reasonable to ask why he has two heads. But the norm is as vaguely defined as the class and we can only say that it is what occurs "on the whole," "for the most part," "other things being equal," and so on. Where measurements are involved, the norm is the arithmetical mean, the average. Where they are not directly involved, it is the mode. These are of course statistical terms and we have no revelation that the world is so constructed that things of the same class must conform to the demands of statistics. It is true that they do but that is because they are usually classified in accordance with some statistical rule.

Moreover, scientists like everyone else inherit their classifications. The men who originally made them often had interests different from those of their heirs. If one is interested mainly in morphology, as the earlier biologists were, one will classify in accordance with morphological likenesses. Things with the same structure will be classified together. But once the time comes when phylogenetic interests prevail over morphological, it turns out that animals and plants which are anatomically similar do not always share the same descent. To take another example, animals used to be classified according to which of the four elements, earth, water, air, and fire, provided their habitat. Hence we had terrestrial animals, aqueous animals, and aerial animals—in fact, in some writers at least one igneous animal, the salamander. This principle gave us the traditional birds, beasts, and fishes. It proved scientifically satisfactory until questions other than those of habitat were raised and at that point bats could no longer be classified with birds nor whales with fishes. But regardless of the principle of classification, we can always say that a deviation is too small to bother with, too exceptional, or within the normal range of variation. In mathematics there is no normal range of variation, for all members of a class are exactly the same.

Questions of policy arise when we want to know what we should do. It is obvious that we can do things only in the future. As long as the future repeats the past, no questions of policy arise. We follow the established routine. No proof is needed that there are some things in nature which occur in repeatable patterns or cycles or rhythms, even though, as in the case of the precession and nutation of the equinoxes, there is a slight annual variation. In such instances we know what we should do; no problem is raised. We simply do what we have always done. The old calendars which gave the work for each month might turn out to be faulty in detail but on the whole they worked fairly well. A farmer living in the Temperate Zone does not have to begin preparing to plant his corn in January, even if January should be unusually warm. He can count on the regularity of the seasons and wait until spring. But when spring finally arrives, he then has to decide when he will plow and plant, for the weather may after all be abnormally cold even though the traditional time for corn-planting has come. If one could imagine a country in which everything was absolutely regular, in which novelty never occurred, no problems of policy would ever worry mankind. The weather, the food supply, the size of the population, would never vary; there would be no rebellion, for everyone would like and dislike the same things and be submissive to custom; no foreigners would ever enter the country nor would natives ever travel abroad to be disturbed by new ideas. Life would be a matter of routine and ritual would take the place of thought. That this is not the situation in which we live—or want to live, perhaps—needs no proof. We know that the sun will rise tomorrow, but we are not sure that it will not be hidden by clouds. And what we should do may depend upon the weather.

Doubts about the future are an integral part of every man's experience and we can only hope that we may plan for its being a repetition of the past. If it were completely unknown and unknowable, we could not even hope and moreover it would be foolish to do any planning at all. The situation is very much like what we find in chess. There are certain well-established routines for opening the game and we can select one and play it. But there are no rules by which we can foresee what our opponent will do to frustrate our opening. There are again fixed rules which determine how a piece may move, but if we could see just which possibilities our opponent would permit us to realize, the game would be over as soon as it began. Such possibilities are determined by him, not by us, and as far as we are concerned, they are a matter of chance. He imposes his decisions upon us and thus limits the range of our moves. The laws of nature might be as well known to us as the rules of chess, but just what combination of circumstances would confront us in the future would be a matter of chance.

There are people who have said that if we knew enough, there would be no such thing as chance, that the word "chance" is a cloak for our ignorance. But "to know enough" would be to know what actually is going to happen and that kind of knowledge can be found only where nothing happens, that is, in logic and mathematics. When we say that a penny must fall either heads up or tails up, we are not dealing with history. We do not have to throw a penny at all to say that much. If only one of two things can happen and we know the names of the two things, we can be very sagacious about the imaginary future. But if before tossing a penny I ask someone, "What is going to turn up?" and am answered, "Either heads or tails," my question has not been answered. As Aristotle once said, It is certain that you will be alive or dead tomorrow, but it is a matter of chance whether you will be alive or dead. It is true that we are in ignorance of what chance will bring forth and in that sense of the phrase chance does cloak our ignorance. But the metaphor of the cloak does not mean that there is no such thing as chance. On the contrary the reason why we are ignorant is because of chance; chance does not exist because of our ignorance.

Chance events occur in the realm of existence where individuals, not universals, are in play. Since rational knowledge cannot handle individuals, for its nature is to deal with classes of things, any event must be a perfect example of a class whose nature is known if its occurrence is to be predictable. Such events are found in laboratories or on paper. The laboratories are so arranged as to eliminate any impurities from the things with which we are dealing. On paper this is not necessary as there we are dealing exclusively with ideas or universals. These impurities are the things which have to be "equal" when we say that such and such an event will occur, other things being equal. They are the symptoms of chance and belong exclusively to the temporal world.

To have devised a technique for purification is one of the great triumphs of the scientific method for it brings the two worlds together as intimately as possible. But it is a triumph bought at the cost of removing reason from experience. The price is not too high to pay, for what we ask of the sciences is an understanding of the general order of events, not a portrait of the world as we live in it. The latter is what we ask of literature and the other arts. The scientist is the man who has sacrificed his personality, his emotional reactions to the problems of policy, the individuality of his experiences, in order to submit himself wholeheartedly to formulating laws which will give us the interrelationships of events. His truths are interpersonal truths. Though they may evoke horror or delight in the minds of those who learn of them, and in his own too when he is not doing science, those emotions are not an integral part of his scientific knowledge.

But works of art are not formulas and always contain an element of the lyrical. That is why we can speak of a painting as "A Giotto," "A Monet," "A Picasso," as if we recognized in each the presence of the man who made it. We may name equations and laws too after the man who discovered or disentangled them, but that is no more than giving a child his father's family name. The importance of Hardy's Law, or Boyle's Law, or Faraday's Law, or Fermat's Last Theorem— assuming it to have been proved—or Gödel's Theorem, is not what it reveals of the men who elaborated it, but what it tells us about some set of facts. But the importance of *Hamlet* or even *The Ancient Mariner* is the part they played both in the lives of their authors and in our own. I am not arguing that one should read *Hamlet* in order to find biographical details concerning Shakespeare; yet one of its values is its reflection of the spirit of a great poet, a single and unique human being. It is true that we can say, if we wish, that *Hamlet* tells us something about the English form of tragedy too and thus tends in the direction of generalization. But it was not written to tell us that, and there is no mention in it of its relation to other tragedies. It is we who use it for that end. An aesthetician or literary critic may read a poem simply as a specimen of a class of poems. We can also deal with our children as biological or psychological specimens, feeling neither love nor hate nor pleasure nor pain nor even remorse or satisfaction.

I am consequently not denying that everything is a member of some class, but at the same time I am insisting that in our vital contact with things we have also to appreciate them as individuals. As such they are unique. Their nature is not exhausted by the class to which reason assigns them, for aside from the multiplicity of classes to which they may legitimately be assigned, they are also part of a flesh-and-blood human being's life. He likes them or dislikes them or feels coldly indifferent to them; he wants them or shuns them; he uses them as instruments to further satisfactions or rejects them as useless; he is frightened by them, puzzled by them, curious about them. He is amazed at their beauty or disgusted by their ugliness. He stands in awe of them like a Stoic beneath the starry sky. And though these verbs and adjectives seem to refer to people and not to things, when we love something or hate something, we form a compound with the thing in question and we do not feel its loveliness or hatefulness to be solely within ourselves. Again, it is theoretically possible to form a science of the things which people in general love and hate, but our love and hate do not depend on our being first drilled in such a science. Just as the planets can move in their elliptical orbits without first studying Newton's *Principia,* so an illiterate savage can beget a child without first taking a course in embryology.

It is perhaps true that if we thoroughly understood everything, we should have no emotions at all. And the literature urging us to subdue our emotions and act only through reason is very great and impressive. But if the lesson were to be so well learned that it would be applied to living, we should be frozen into inactivity. For reason stops short when confronted with individuals; the most it can do is to invent a proper name of them. A glass of water is not simply a chemical specimen: it is this glass of water here and now, which I need to quench my thirst, which I will give up to someone who needs it more than I do or which I shall hastily swallow before he sees it, which will keep me going for a few more hours, and what do I care whether it is a compound of molecules made up of two gases or not? If I am thirsty, science will tell me that water will quench my thirst, but it will not produce the water, nor tell me whether I should drink it myself or give it to someone else, or alleviate the pangs of my conscience if I do drink it instead of sharing it with my companions.

A man in the desert can always tell himself that it makes little difference whether he survives or dies of thirst and, insofar as he is simply one specimen of the species *homo sapiens,* it clearly does not. He can say that all things die and why not he? But he knows that he is more than a biological specimen: he is an individual human being with a strong desire to survive and, though he may also believe that he has no more reason to survive than the millions who have already died, his desire takes precedence over his reason and he will make every effort to save his life regardless of what reason tells him. He will, if he has enough strength, maintain that he is not on this earth to exemplify a scientific thesis; it is the task of science to deal with him. If he suddenly thinks of the general custom of self-preservation, he may simply in order to defy the custom decide not to survive. And if someone later explains his death on the grounds of altruism or self-hatred or a wish for *post-mortem* glory or fatigue or desperation, he himself will simply have demonstrated how no individual is a perfect example of any abstract class.

If "existence" is a predicate[2] and there is a legitimate dif-

2 The question of whether "existence" is a predicate was popularized

ference between the idea of humanity and living human beings, then one can no more infer the existence of human beings from the idea of humanity than one can infer the existence of mermaids from the image of them handed down from ancient times. What is implicit in an idea is always another idea and there is no necessary factual truth in any logical deduction. "Existence" as a predicate is a logical surd, not indefinable to be sure, but not deducible. This is presumably what the existentialists mean when they say that it is prior to essence. When we say that mermaids do not exist we have a more or less clear idea of what we are talking about. "More or less," since the meaning of ideas is in part determined by the people who have them and in part by tradition. But in any event a person who says that mermaids do not exist could reasonably be asked to say why not. However bad his evidence, it will be based upon tests for existence which are not identical with tests for signification: he can have both a clear idea of what a mermaid would be if mermaids did exist and also maintain that they do not exist. Presumably he would first give a thorough description of the anatomy and physiology of a mermaid and then logically demonstrate that such an organism was not viable. But if after his demonstration he should actually see a mermaid, all his logic would fall to pieces and, if he was a zealous philosopher, he would then pick up the pieces and see why they failed to hold together. We are then in the curious situation of being able to demonstrate nonexistence and forced to observe or experience existence.

Existence then as a logical surd can never be deduced except

by Immanuel Kant when he asked what was the difference between an idea of something and that of which it was the idea, for instance, what is the difference between our idea of a ten-dollar bill and an existing ten-dollar bill. This is a distinction which most of us feel that we understand, but to define it has proved an obstacle to most philosophers. Yet if we say that "existence" is a predicate differentiating two kinds of ten-dollar bills, we ought to be able to define the difference. If William James were here to answer, he would give the so-called pragmatic answer, "You can spend an existent bill." But that would do only for currency. Furthermore, pragmatic tests can be made only by existent human beings, so that the problem has only been pushed back a step.

tautologically. That is, we can lay down the conditions of existence and from them conclude that certain things exist. And obviously if we find certain existent things, we can argue back to the previous existence of their causes or determinants. But otherwise existent things must be found in our experience in some sense of that ambiguous term, must be observed, encountered, perceived. If this were not so, any idea or image fabricated by the human mind would be proved to have exemplifications in the spatio-temporal world. But we know that this is not the case. If this leads to the erection of two or more worlds, so much the worse for simplicity. I am pleading neither for nor against a multiplicity of worlds. In fact, the very notion of a world of experience, a world of dreams, a world of ideas, needs intensive clarification. We have experience of things, dreams, and ideas, but to establish each as a world on the model of the solar system or something of that sort seems unwarranted. For it might be thought that a world would be self-enclosed with only external relations to other worlds. Ideas, dreams, things, images, emotions, are all so mixed up together in the general jumble of life that a long treatise would be needed to sort them out. Be that as it may, many of our vital problems arise from the conflict between our ideas and our perceptions, or, if the phrase be preferred, between essence and existence. It is analogous to the conflict between what we want to do and what we can do. We can desire even the impossible. And sometimes—witness aviation—such a desire becomes fulfilled.

That we actually have an inner life of dreams, meditations, simple thoughts, a stream of consciousness which does not conform to what we find in our outer life, can be taken for granted. The words "inner" and "outer" are an unhappy metaphor and it might be better to substitute adjectives such as "private" and "public" or "personal" and "interpersonal." Since the beginnings of scientific psychology it has been the aim of its practitioners to find some way of externalizing what goes on "within the mind," so that general laws concerning its behavior may be formulated. Sometimes this aim has landed the psychologist in a position of denying the very existence of those problems which he has been attempting to solve. It may, for instance, be profitable to correlate certain kinds of behavior, whether those of the muscles and glands or those of the total human body, with the various psychical events in which we are interested. This sort of exercise had its heyday in the period when physiological psychology was in fashion. In physics it has proved profitable to correlate the tone, pitch, and timbre of sounds with the traits of air waves, or vibrations in some other medium. But just as the characters of the waves are not identical with the sounds, though they are the one controllable condition of our hearing anything, so the behavior in question would not be identical with the dream, the image, the emotion, or whatever psychical event might be of interest to the scientist.

If it is assumed that there is nothing in the world except physico-chemical substances and their configurations, then of course it would be nonsensical to argue for the existence of minds which are not physico-chemical. The mere existence of minds would not prevent there being a scientific psychology as long as all items in the mental world were sufficiently homogeneous for general terms to name them and also if they were related in such a way that constant laws could be framed to describe them. But one of the features of an inner life is its being the possession of a person who feels intensely his uniqueness, his peculiarity, and hence his solitude. There is always the possibility that our most personal experiences are common to others, but there is no way of discovering this. The sting of our solitude is not the fact that we are self-enclosed, but the feeling that we are self-enclosed.

Most of us would agree with Landor's girl in the poem,

> O, if you felt the pain I feel!
> But O, who ever felt as I?

That this can be phrased as a rhetorical question is important. For like all such questions, the answer is "understood." The matter is not simply that no two people experience a single feeling together, that my heartache is not yours, but that the kind of heartache which I have is my kind of heartache and no one else's. I may, if I am a lyric poet or simply given to expatiating upon my troubles, attempt to communicate my feelings to you and I may also succeed in arousing pity, if not sympathy, of a sort in you.

But even if I could transfer my heartache to you, as one might pass a cup of coffee to someone else, the very fact that it had been detached from me would alter it. For the *me* in this case is all my past, my associations with others, my own sense of failure, my hurt pride, my faulty estimate of the person who caused the pain. No one can share these things with me for they are what constitutes in part my whole personality. Moreover, the very fact that I have turned my heartache into a poem or a commonplace speech about it has modified it. Indeed it may be an alleviation of it or the very antithesis, an intensification of it.

But were reason to handle this, it would first of all demand a univalent vocabulary to name the feelings under discussion. Pleasure and pain, anger, despair, joy, and the other emotions would have to be exactly the same, whether I were experiencing them or you. The rational man would reply to Landor's girl, "Tell me precisely what your pain is and I will tell you whether anyone else has ever felt it or not." If amenable to persuasion, she might then embark on the futile search for the right name of her pain. She would end up with rough labels and actually in the poem the best she could do was to indicate her physical state: "My fingers ache, my lips are dry." But one's fingers can ache and one's lips can be dry from a dozen different causes, and it is very likely that what emotional power is in the poem comes from Landor's willingness not to be specific. As a matter of fact it is better to do a bit of introspection and to try to tell someone else of one's feelings, let us say of pleasure, than to deal with an imaginary case. Before one is aware of it one makes a distinction between the pleasures of eating and drinking, of sport, of reading, of conversation, of daydreaming, and so on, and then these too become subdivided into varieties, and finally one comes out with a slightly different pleasure for each experience which is pleasurable.

This is an old theme in hedonistic philosophies which distinguish between higher and lower pleasures, bodily and spiritual pleasures, sensory and intellectual pleasures, egoistic and altruistic pleasures. Such philosophies recognize that the term "pleasure" in itself is much too broad to be useful. There is nothing mysterious in the need for such minute differentiation. We all know that we like some things more than others and, though we may call our attitude "liking," our liking for pictures is not equivalent to our liking for friends. It would perhaps be otiose to expand upon this theme. Hence we shall simply assert that both the object of our emotions and our total personality, whether harmonious or in a state of conflict, determine what the emotion will be. Insofar as these are unique, they are logical surds and any attempt at explaining them, like all attempts at explanation, will be dependent upon abstracting from them precisely what makes them unique.

Added to this is that aspect of life which retains the past and anticipates the future. In rational discourse, logic, the temporal dimension disappears, as we have said. The rocks of a million or two years ago are the same as the rocks of today insofar as they are subject to geological laws. In the sciences the past is retained without change and that is why a geologist can tell us more or less what happened to the earth in the very distant past. But our memory does not retain the past exactly as it was but transforms it. Not only is memory selective but it is also prejudiced. This can be verified by asking three or four people to testify to their recollection of a public event in which they have all participated. What they remember of it and the way in which it is reported will vary significantly. We may contrast our strains of memory with the public record, if we will, and think of the latter as a check on the former. But this too is a falsification of the facts since the record also has been filtered through the minds of recorders. We need not, however, go into that, for all we need for our present purposes is evidence of discrepancy and that is not lacking.

Furthermore, the past as it is remembered, regardless of what it actually was, is present; that is, it is represented in our minds by a memory-image now before us. That image may have the quality of "pastness" attached to it and we know that what it stands for is over and done with. But it itself is here and now and just as it has never appeared before, so it will never appear again. We can again subtract from it all those accretions of sentiment and novelty which dwelling upon it may produce and we may think of it simply in terms of what it stands for. But once more we are disfiguring it seriously in order to discuss it rationally. We try to think of our memory as a series of events which have floated off from us and are being recaptured, as if we had long-handled nets which we could toss as far backwards as we wish and snare whatever we wish. But this way of thinking distorts what happens, since we in part determine what we can see to snare and what we catch changes as we catch it. Moreover, we are not always able to remember what we think we should like to recall and what we forget is often forgotten in spite of our desire to remember it. Freud has shown reason for believing that we often misrepresent such a desire and that we wish to forget what we forget more often than we wish to recall it. Whether his reasons will stand up under criticism, I do not know, but surely the stubborn resistance of certain past experiences to recollection is so common an experience that one may well ask what the block is. And we might also ask why other experiences linger stubbornly in our memory in spite of our desire to forget them. Our inner life seems to be as resistant to volition as the physical world is.

In logic we have an order of priority and posteriority, the order which runs from premises to conclusions. But a glance at that order will suffice to show how misleading it would be to confuse logical and chronological order. In formal reasoning the conclusion is implicit in the premises and needs only to be drawn out of them. This process, as we perform it, is to be sure temporal. But there is no process in a series of equations; there is only a static pattern. When we are reasoning not from equations, which are tautologies, but from major and minor premises as in a syllogism or from established relationships whose transitivity, symmetricality, or lack of them, we know beforehand, we are still speaking figuratively when we speak of priority and posteriority. We shall not dogmatize about the rules of logic, but the fact remains that if what is in the premises reappears in the conclusion, it must be self-identical all the way. This is essential if reasoning is to be valid, that is, consistent.

What can such a technique of thinking do with a series of items which change from moment to moment? In memory we use the same name for that which is remembered and for our memory of it. But, as we have said, the two things are vastly different. My memory of my boyhood is not my boyhood and in all probability, if I could actually lay one beside the other, I would be astonished at their differences. If every time a word was used, it shifted its meaning according to the context in which it occurred, one would have an analogous situation in reasoning. One may say that the major variations in the re-membered past are the emotional auras which surround it. That may be true. But those emotional auras are an integral part of a memory and when they are removed, nothing is left but a faint image of a material object or group of objects.

I can recall much of the multiplication table without a severe emotional shock; but I cannot recall my first day at school in cold objectivity. That it was a first day made it dif-ferent from all other days, not simply in that it had a peculiar ordinal number attached to it, but in that it involved fright, fear of the unknown, a severance of family relations, hostile and suspicious eyes, the warm smile of a teacher against the mocking leer of the older boys, the smell of unwashed children, blackboards gray with chalk dust, in short a grand mishmash of what I projected into the scene and what was impressed upon me by it. Not all boys are terrified by their first day at school; not all children smell; not all teachers smile. There may be some plausible generalization about first days at school, for all I know, but none of them would be more than the faintest picture of what any real boy feels on his first day at school. If my own memory of my first day is so vivid, it is because of the kind of child I was, not because of the school. If I can even now toward the end of my life recall that scene with revulsion, I can only conclude that I must have been unusually timid, cowardly, shy, or otherwise incapable of facing novelty. Or it may well be that my memory is at fault and that I have invested the experience with qualities which it did not actually have.

Reason did not create the memory which I now have of that event though it may well correct it. There was probably little real hostility on the part of the other children, little maleficence on the part of my parents who sent me to school, little cause for fright. It is even more unreasonable that a man in his late sixties should look back upon that day with something of the horror which he now thinks he felt when the day was being lived through. If the horror at that time grew out of the feeling of being rejected by my mother, that only fortifies the argument. If I had that feeling, I no longer have any cause to have it. If I had or have an abnormal sense of self-pity, that might explain it in very general terms, but it would also imply that self-pity can determine what one remembers and what one forgets as well as fix the emotional tone of memories. And since, to repeat once again, my memory of that day is not the day itself, the most that reason can do is to influence my attitude toward my memory, so that the next time I think of it, it may have changed its color. In other words, I have to adopt a proposition of policy toward something which is present in order to change my future behavior. But the very fact that I am confronted with this problem shows that the name which I give to my memory-image is not univalent.

Our hopes for the future are also an important part of our

experience for, unless we live ritualistically, always doing the same thing over and over again, habit will not guide us. Much of what we do is habitual and I am not denying that. But in most lives the future is different from the past not simply in date but in the kind of problem to which it gives rise. In spite of proverbial philosophy, we simply cannot be prepared for everything. We can be prepared only for that which we anticipate. And we can fruitfully anticipate only that which we have already experienced or of course the past with slight modifications. If that which is entirely unknown or which has never come within the range of our experience occurs, then we are helpless and all the reason in the world will be of no aid. We handle some incidents through what we have read of others doing in similar circumstances; we sometimes make a lucky guess and meet the unanticipated head-on without disaster; but we cannot conceivably prepare for the totally novel. If we live in New England, we do not have to be prepared to meet earthquakes, though earthquakes have been known to occur in New England. If we live in California, it is prudent to build an earthquake-resistant house, even though no earthquake may occur. This is just common sense. But the reason why it is sensible is that there is at least some likelihood of earthquakes in California and very little in New England.

Some of us can remember the days before 1914 when the possibility of a war seemed so remote that the experts, even after it had broken out, argued that it could not last very long. When it was finally over, most of us thought that its horrors were such that no nation would ever go to war again. Twenty years later the same nations were trying to exterminate one another in an even more horrible manner. This second war lasted for six years and was a hellish nightmare. Most of us have seen the senselessness of starting a third war. Nevertheless all preparations are being made for it. The third, if fought with modern weapons, whether thermonuclear bombs, disease germs, intercontinental missiles, or some secret weapon more effective than these, will exceed in frightfulness the second.

Reason would tell us to make any sacrifice in order to avoid it. But our method of avoiding it is to prepare for it. I imagine that the leaders on both sides feel that something unpredictable may happen to lessen its loathsomeness, to permit the survival of the victor—for it is of course believed that there will be a victor—and to prevent future causes of a fourth war. I imagine this. But the only ground for such an image is what we have learned from the past. We cannot imagine a world which is so unlike the past that our reasoning powers cannot lay down a policy for living in it. We cannot imagine a race of men so deformed by radiation that it will be unviable. We cannot imagine a world in which only the savages in the heart of Africa will be alive. But, it will be said, you are imagining such things now as you write them. Yes, the words are being typed on paper, but were I to attempt to construct the kind of life which would be prevalent, I doubt whether my imagination could possibly do. more than project into the future what I have read in books on cultural anthropology. And such books are descriptive, not prophetic.

It is the very essence of hope to be unreasonable. It was not reasonable in 1775 to think that the American colonists could win their independence. It was not reasonable in 1940 after Dunkirk to think that the British could survive. It was not reasonable in 1945 to think that they would withdraw from India. It was not reasonable in the Age of the Great Reptiles to think that they would disappear and that the mammals would take over. It is not reasonable now to think that the 815,000 species of arthropods will conquer the 3,500 species of mammals and that the day will come when spiders, crustaceans, and insects will rule the earth. It was not reasonable in 1930 to think that the most highly educated nation in Europe would kiss the feet of a psychopath and his gang and follow him blindly wherever he led them. Such thoughts are not reasonable simply because they deal with events for which there is no precedent. Reason can announce that the same causes are followed by the same effects. But first we have to detect the causes and second we have to be sure that they are really the same. Identity is found in the realm of eternity, not in history.

The justification for hope is precisely its unreasonableness. The world ought always to be the same. There ought always to be rigid obedience to natural law, as there is in a laboratory. But we have discovered that the world is not a laboratory and that events are wayward. If we could foresee the future, hope would be a waste of time. We should then know all that is going to happen including what is going to happen to us. Not being able to predict accurately, we hope for the best. And the best is that the future will satisfy our present desires. It is not impossible to discover the ways in which any desire can be satisfied, but these are conditions the existence of which will not come about through our efforts except by accident. For many of them reside in the will of other people whose co-operation is needed if we are to get what we want.

I can think of no value which can be achieved by unaided effort. Whether the value be salvation or goodness or justice or beauty or health, to say nothing of the economic values, we can get them only with the aid of others. We can of course plan ways of securing their co-operation, and society has been in-genious in so organizing itself that there are specialists who provide satisfaction for almost everyone. But there is no point in minimizing the will of some to obstruct the purposes of others. Such people need not be criminals. They may simply be people who believe that the past is good enough or that God wants His children to suffer. It is safe to say that every innova-tion in culture, even in literature and the other arts, even in scientific investigation and technological invention, has met with resistance. Social tradition can be understood, for its persistence renders it intelligible. Tradition is one of our ways of defeating time. If there were such a thing as a purely tradi-tional society, hope would be silly. We might idly dream of a future different from the past, but we could not hope for its realization.

The dominant forces of society seem never to have opposed the formation of hope for a better life after death. As long as heavenly felicity is confined to heaven, no one will object. The objections are voiced and implemented when one begins "to build Jerusalem in England's green and pleasant land." For man as a rational animal cannot tolerate a change so radical that earth would become unrecognizable. The ground would grow soft beneath our feet and we should flounder about as if in sticky mud. We need stability if only for the sake of understanding things. As long as the dreamer projects his hopes into a distant future, distant enough not to threaten the safety of society, he will be allowed to dream. Trouble comes when his hopes fasten on tomorrow. Then he is likely to form a little society of his own, all of whose members, he hopes, will co-operate to realize a plan which he has devised. There will always be a surrogate for a collective mind in the statutes and traditions of a state; but it is always a mind resting uneasily beneath the threat of disintegration. For as societies have developed in the industrial era where urban life has brought people of many and diverse interests together, they have split into subsocial groups each of which has a purpose which may be hostile to tradition. It may begin simply as a collective attempt to bring to fruition some hope which others have not thought of. I suppose that the Society for the Prevention of Cruelty to Animals was such a group. But as it grows and its program wins adherents, it tends to conflict with the programs of other social groups: the S.P.C.A., for instance, began to preach against the use of animals for experimental purposes; antivivisection bills were introduced into the state legislatures; and before long the scientific community had to fight back. Only monsters want to be cruel to any living thing, but the biologist, the pharmacologist, the surgeon want also to find out something about the reaction of living organisms to certain drugs, the possibility of performing certain operations, the general economy of mammalian physiology. If the animalitarian had his way, this scientific work would be blocked. If the scientists have their way, the animalitarian is blocked. The United States has seen this sort of evolution in dozens of cases: witness the Woman's Christian Temperance Union, the Abolitionists, woman-suffrage groups, and now the movement for racial desegregation.

Rationally society is a unit. Anthropologists study its structure as if it had a single structure: one recalls the late Ruth Benedict's *Patterns of Culture*. Nationalistic propagandists outline its purpose: think of "The American Way of Life." Businessman and industrialists, with the help of psychological warriors, play up the general needs: everyone has to have a telephone and an automobile and sometimes two of each. Even the 180-odd Christian sects say that they are all Christians and that they "fundamentally" all believe in the same thing. But every society has its recalcitrant members and in the United States the various forms of recalcitrancy express themselves in social organizations.

The one pervasive trait of Americans is a kind of tolerance, though often attenuated, of diversity. The number of automobiles and telephones far exceeds the need for them and most have become a nuisance, the former a hazard to life, the latter to tranquillity. If Catholicism is Christian, then Unitarianism is not. Yet such diversities are tolerated, for Americans themselves are dependent on the tolerance of others for them. Every group is originally organized to achieve some goal, hope of which presumably is shared by its members. But sometimes when the goal is achieved the group lives on for self-perpetuation. And sometimes when the goal cannot be achieved, the group fights all the harder to achieve it. It may well be that it is more important for the human psyche to have hopes than to have them realized, as Lessing believed that the search for truth was more important than its attainment. Rationally it is foolish to hope for the impossible. But it is nevertheless at the heart of humanity.

The two other theological virtues, charity and faith, are in much the same situation. How can one argue another man into having charity? A man either loves his brother or he does not. He may be convinced that he ought to act as if he loved him, to contribute to his comfort and health, to send money to him, but it has not required my typewriter to point out that the act and the feeling which are supposed to stimulate it are two different things. One may agree on grounds of self-interest, or the general good, or the greatest happiness of the greatest number, or some other ethical principle, that the deeds which would flow out of charity, if one had charity, should be performed. But that may lead more to annoyance than to charity. Love, whether of one's neighbor or of oneself, is something which arises in one without thought. Even if I do not love my neighbor, I need not harm him. But the fact that I do not harm him surely does not mean that I love him. And the moment that rational grounds are given for love, even for sexual love, it evaporates.

Love creates its own motivation, its own grounds, its own principles of justification. Few things in history have proved more disastrous to the individuals involved than Antony's love for Cleopatra. Is anyone so naïve as to believe that Antony could have been argued out of it? In countries, like the United States, where marriages are made by a man and a woman on the simple grounds that they want to get married, how many parents have tried to point out their unreasonableness to them? And in countries where marriages are "arranged," how much love is awakened by the arrangements? On a less intimate plane, how many teachers have failed in their efforts to induce in their students a love for the subjects which are required for a diploma? And how futile has argument been when applied to the curing of bad habits! The discrepancy between the books of the ethicists, such as Bentham on the one hand and Kant on the other, and the books of the moralists, such as La Rochefoucauld or Vauvenargues, accentuates this. The former deal with eternal man, the latter with historical.

The gap in this field between the two is of a certain theoretical interest. For as soon as man's moral behavior is described as it is, rather than as it ought to be, the description appears to be intolerably cynical. Yet one can describe the behavior of the social animals toward one another, even that of the social insects, and it seems admirable rather than disgraceful. From the days of the ancients, the fidelity, chastity, industry, and lawfulness of certain beasts have been dwelt upon even when they were mythological. The most striking example of this is found in the medieval bestiaries where the beasts are used as moral and religious exemplars. Yet the very men who wrote such tales also believed that the animals were irrational. Sometimes the admiration which the writers had for them was based on the idea that they were more "natural" than men and that if men would turn to nature and away from art, they too would be more noble and decent. Sometimes their edifying behavior was seen as God's reason acting through them, and God's reason becomes a law of nature. Paradoxically enough, they demand of human reason that it make men act like the beasts, in a uniform and regular manner. Reason should, they seem to be saying, lay down universal laws so that all men would behave in the same way on the same occasions. But what would this be other than to turn reason into instinct? It makes little sense to praise the elephant, one of the usual exemplars, for its chastity if it is chaste because it has no inclination to be unchaste. It makes less sense to praise the worker bee for working, since there is nothing else that it can do anyway. One might as well praise men for walking on two feet instead of on all fours. Moral victory is a victory over nature—or instinct; it is doing what you do not want to do, making your individual desires conform to a set of laws. Books on ethics which tell their readers what they ought to do usually end up by telling them that they ought not to be what they are.

This is a pathetic attempt to pull time and eternity together, to iron out the inherent differences in individuals as if men and women were above all else specimens of some scientific class of substances. That the differences persist in spite of all inducements to conform is proof enough that they are in-eradicable. Rewards and punishments, both terrestrial and celestial, have obviously not brought about that smoothness of behavior which the ethicists want. Ethicists emphasize the difference between what they call the *ought* and the *is,* between fact and value, and some have even gone so far as to say that the good is precisely that which never is but ought to be. It is an ever-retreating ideal which once attained would cease to be good.

Such a result is the identification of values with mathematical beings whose purity seems to remove them from the dirt of daily life. But we know now that these objects of mathematics are generated by the imagination of the mathematician or, if one prefer, by convention. Anything may be expected of a science whose first principles are tautologies, except that it be applicable to the world of experience. Let us suppose that we have a kind of intellectual intuition which puts us in contact with these crystalline beings, or that they are revealed to us by a supernatural source. They are still beyond the grasp of reason. And if we switch from mathematics to moral values, we are no better off and each ethical system becomes a web of logical implications with no necessary efficacy for existence. Moreover, it will be the intuited first principles which will vitalize the system, not the inferences drawn from them.

The very fact that we are called upon to find our ethical premises through intuition accentuates the difficulty of finding any which will be generally acceptable. We can of course through scientific investigation find what men on the whole desire, utilize as standards of good and evil, and at times attempt to conform to. But this would be brushed aside by the ethicist as sociology or anthropology. Sociological generalizations, no matter how well grounded, would be said to have no moral relevance. And it must be granted that there are occasions on which a man refuses to accept the most general laws of his tribe. He may be punished for his recalcitrancy, but he will insist that there are laws which are higher than those of the state. The ultimate triumph of Christianity was attributable as much to the stubborn recalcitrancy of the saints and martyrs as to either the reasonableness of the doctrines in which they believed or the political organization of the Church. The gradual reform of punitive justice in the state was equally due to the refusal on the part of individuals to accept its harshness. The ability to say *No* to the consensus in moral questions is surely nothing than can either be depreciated or qualified as futile. We may feel that punitive justice is too lenient, that paganism was as sound a religion as Christianity, but we still cannot deny that both were reformed by people, not by some natural evolutionary law. If we agree with the reforms, and most Occidentals do agree with them, then we have to grant that a nonrational act took precedence over the reason. And we also have to grant that if it makes sense to say that there is such a thing as ethical truth, it can be discovered by an insight which is not rational.

But a similar state of affairs will be found in any field concerned with values. There is no more rational truth in Italian Renaissance painting than in medieval painting, in modern architecture than in Gothic, in Schönberg than in Mozart. It may not be good usage to speak of artistic truth, and I should be willing to agree with that opinion, but whatever the judgment of aesthetic value may be based upon, its basis is not reason, if reason means logic. It cannot be denied that when certain artistic rules have been widely accepted, there will always be artists who will find their satisfaction in adhering to them. But the history of the arts shows that every once in a while a man appears who rejects them, either as a whole or in part. Beethoven cannot be explained exclusively on his conformity to the procedures of Haydn, nor can Delacroix be explained as a faithful student even of Rubens, though in both cases what is called the influence of their teachers is clear.

But if there is really a right and a wrong way to paint or to compose music, then it is folly to pretend that the man who refuses to follow the right way is nevertheless right. His in-novations may become the rule after he has won recognition, but they are still innovations. He or his disciples may maintain that he is right and all his predecessors wrong. But his rightness is not the kind of rightness which appears in the work of such men as Copernicus, Galileo, or Newton. It consists in its being accepted and in nothing more. Again, a psychologist or sociolo-gist might be able to explain why it gained general acceptance, but that would be the answer to a different question.

Moreover, when a man has come to the moment when he can no longer say *Yes*, he does not refuse to assent through argument. He may argue about his rightness afterward, as a lawyer defends his client knowing perfectly well that the ac-cused did whatever he did without any thought whatsoever. The man who strikes a blow in passion is behaving like the poet who is blinded by a sudden flash of insight. The flash may vary in intensity. It may be merely a faint glow produced by a single line which emerges into his consciousness. It may be a rhythm of verse without much in the way of words. It may be a group of verses or a brilliant metaphor or an incident. But whatever it is, it appears suddenly and becomes the nucleus of his work of art, a cell which divides and grows until a com-pleted poem is formed from it. This is of course the contribu-tion of his unconscious, not the whole work of art but its heart. Later on, in retrospection, the artist may be able to understand what produced that central nucleus, just as the passionate man when his passion has cooled may be able to recollect what set him aflame. But to maintain that a man's recollection of an act and its cause are identical with the act as it is being per-formed is a manifest distortion of the facts.

A number of different premises may imply the same con-clusion as far as logic is concerned. In a hypothetical argument one can never infer the antecedent from the conclusion. Simi-larly in history one can never infer the cause from the effect. We have to distinguish between the structure of exposition (logic) and that of discovery (history) and it is notorious that no one has yet succeeded in formalizing the pattern of discovery. Induction has been the stumbling block of all logicians and we have now reached the point of maintaining that deduction is always tautologous. To repeat the same meaning in different words is not a trivial game for it may at a minimum lead to clarification. Nor would anyone deny that the annihilation of obscurity is a good. But to confuse exposition with discovery is absurd. Men knew that the earth was spherical long before Magellan's time, but who would identify the circumnavigation of the globe with the deductive proof that it must be round?

Our failure to superimpose the world of logic upon the world of history and make the two fit is due to the existence of time. Logic being timeless can give us only a fixed pattern of immutable objects, whereas the very essence of temporal beings is never to be the same from moment to moment. Moreover, the world we live in seems to include no universals, whereas the world we reason about has no individuals. Yet it is the former which provides the problems which the latter tries to solve and is the testing ground for its answers. And in the final analysis it provides those basic metaphors by means of which we build up satisfactory explanations of events.

3
Basic Metaphors

EVER SINCE THE PUBLICATION OF VAIHINGER'S
Philosophie des Als-Ob (The Philosophy of the As-If), philosophers have become more and more conscious of fictions
and of their use in rational discourse. Among such fictions are
metaphors (or similes) which occur especially in general explanations of large groups of events. Professor S. C. Pepper has
attemped to classify them under four heads in his *World-
Hypotheses:* mechanism, "formism," organicism, and con-
textualism. The point of view of the present essay is that the
number of basic metaphors is not limited to four and that, as
far as anyone knows, a scientist or philosopher may adopt any
figure of speech which he finds illuminating and use it as
widely as he chooses.

For instance, in the post-Kantians and especially in Schelling, the notion of polarity was basic. Without attempting to
define a literal statement, since all assertions contain a figurative element, let us say that literally polar opposites are determined by their positions in space. If Cartesian co-ordinates
are set up in a plane, then for every point with a positive sign
there will be another point with a negative sign corresponding
to it, just as in the series of integers for every positive number
there is a corresponding negative number. If then a line stands
for a direction in space, for every point on the line moving, let
us say, to the right, there will be a corresponding point moving
to the left. By settling upon some point as *zero,* the opposite
points can be easily determined.

In ordinary common-sense speech we have such terms as "to the right" and "to the left," "clockwise" and "anticlockwise," "up" and "down," and so on. If we say that these expressions and those similar to them are the literal bases of the notion of opposition, then polarity is a metaphor derived from our experience of things arranged in space, as the original meaning of the words "opposition" or "antithesis" would suggest.

No one knows, nor can anyone find out, how the notion of opposition arose. But one can speculate that like so many other basic metaphors it grew out of a human experience so common and perhaps so impressive that it was projected into the world beyond us. We read into opposition a kind of hostility; we speak of opposing forces, as if we were facing an enemy moving toward us; we realize the impossibility of doing both of two opposite things at the same time, just as we discover that we cannot move in two opposite directions as the same time. Surely one of the most striking experiences of the child must be frustration, though it is likely that children differ in their sensitivity to obstacles, just as adults do. Why we should translate frustration into spatial terms is problematic, though it is at least probable that our inability to do more than reach for things when we are infants is the cause of this. But all this is speculation.

For a man like Schelling polarity had a more extensive meaning. To say that males and females are polar opposites, as he did, is clearly not to say that men are set down in a position in space which is opposite to the position of females. To speak of the contradictory of a proposition as the polar opposite of the proposition which it contradicts, is again not to say that it has any position in space whatsoever. To speak of light as the opposite of darkness, of red as the opposite of green, of the *Vernunft* as the opposite of the *Verstand,* of the Romantic as the opposite of the Classic, of the tragic as the opposite of the comic, of mind as the opposite of matter, is to add something to what we have imagined to be the literal meaning of opposition. We cannot be sure of just what this something is in each case, but sometimes the two opposites would seem to be mutually exclusive classes belonging to the same genus, as men and women are both human beings but no man is a woman. At times the emphasis seems to be on the complementarity of the two classes, as red is the color complementary to green, the two when mixed giving one a gray. At times there seems to be a kind of antagonism between the two opposites, as if they stood for the champions of two opposing armies drawn up and facing each other. And at times they seem to be pointing to the interdependence of the two opposites which together form a whole. Thus when Kant said that percepts were blind without concepts and concepts empty without percepts, he was presumably trying to point out that knowledge as a whole depended on the knowers' having both, purely perceptual knowledge being inarticulate, purely conceptual having no existential reference.

If our suggestion of the literal meaning of opposition is correct, then these added meanings are metaphorical. Men and women are opposites in no literal sense at all and, though someone might say that psychologically the sexual differentiation is a matter of the two ends of a scale, a matter of degree, it would still be true that the two extremes of the scale would have to be distinguished in such a way that no man would be a woman and yet both men and women would belong to the same species of animal. This, however, would not be the whole story. It would land one in asserting merely that the two classes were what Aristotle called contraries and not necessarily contradictories. Most logicians would agree, I think, that no term in itself is the contradictory of any other; contradiction obtains between sentences. Hence if one wanted to set up pairs of opposites, one would have to find additional attributes, in this case of masculinity and femininity, such that they would individually "imply" the exclusion of others. To revert now to popular sexual mythology, one would say that women are passive and men active, women intuitive and men rational, women artistic and men scientific, women sensitive and men thick-skinned. And each of these attributes would be so conceived that if a person possessed one of each pair, he could not possibly possess the other. This example is to be sure nonsense, as anyone likely to read these words will see at once, but people have nevertheless used them as identifying characters even when they have spoken of them as "tendencies." A tendency is a movement, incipient or actual, in a direction. Its use too is metaphorical. It is introduced into a scientific or philosophic theory when the framer of the theory wishes to include a dynamic factor into his universe, that is, when he is not exclusively interested in the morphology of his world. There is no inherent dynamism in polarity. The North and South Poles are opposite each other but not engaged in a struggle against each other. But the metaphor of opposition as it is usually employed includes the element of antagonism. One opposite is the potential enemy of the other; it presents something to be overcome or something which may overcome itself. Victory and defeat seem to be uppermost in the minds of men who use this metaphor, though at times, as in the case of Hegel, both parties are said to be elevated to a superior plane by the reconciliation of opposites.

Another and quite different basic metaphor is that of law. If laws are simply generalized descriptions, the metaphorical element is attenuated. All generalizations, however, have to be based on classifications and all classifications are based on comparisons which in turn are based on recognized similarities. Insofar as something is thought of as a member of a class, then it is thought of as being like some other things. This is incontrovertible. But law in this sense is vastly different from law in the sense of a command to do something or a prohibition. The Ten Commandments are laws in this second sense. But from the early days of the history of philosophy a confusion was made between laws as descriptions and laws as commands. The confusion appears most clearly in those philosophies which argue from the existence of law to the existence of a lawgiver. The *Hymn to Zeus* of Cleanthes is a good example of this way of thinking. Here God is required as a lawgiver, much as in Newton's *General Scholium* or in the Duke of Argyll's *The Reign of Law*. To such authors it was unthinkable that a collection of things and events could behave in a uniform manner unless there was a single legislator ordering them to do so. No use is made of this metaphor in the deductions which Newton drew in the body of the *Principia;* the existence of the divine legislator is itself a deduction from the universality of the Law of Gravitation. But in Stoicism the divine order took on a moral complexion and the whole duty of man consisted in obedience to universal law.

The idea of obedience to law, or of the control exercised by law upon things, suggests again that this is a metaphor derived from personal experience. Just as we reach for distant things and are frustrated, so at a very early age we become accustomed to being ordered about, told what to do and what not to do. It is not until we reach adolescence that we can even begin to satisfy our desires without subterfuge. Submission to higher powers is the rule. And even when we are rebellious, we rebel against a rule of which we are only too conscious. We do not reward and punish ourselves except indirectly; we are rewarded and punished by others. Insofar as these others are consistent, they establish uniform rules of behavior and their goal seems to be the creation of a little world in which everyone acts like everyone else. Ironically enough, the legislators themselves are often frustrated, not only by their subjects but also by the inevitable changes in cultural history. They then comfort themselves by looking backward to their own childhood when they were good and obedient as all children were. By instilling in their subjects the notion of unalterable law, they make it possible for them also to project obedience to the same kind of regulation into a world which can be neither punished nor rewarded.

The suspicion that there might be one or a few consistent laws governing the universe made itself felt when philosophers turned away from polytheism to monotheism. Paganism in the

Mediterranean basin moved in the direction of syncretism, the local gods becoming fused into one god, sometimes to an absurd extent, as in the case of Kronos, Saturn, and Moloch. It is likely that all people have one supreme god, if they have any gods at all, for the constitution of heaven usually copies that of earth. Now the very idea of a cosmos is based on the hypothesis that everything manifests order and the differences between the various schools of philosophy turn upon their answers to the question of what kind of order it manifests and of how simple it is.

The two orders which were most frequently advanced are that of mechanical causal law and that of teleology. The second is clearly metaphorical, for no one would say that the purposes of human beings are identical with those of planets, falling stones, and growing plants, though Aristotle came close to saying that when he identified purposive behavior with regular behavior. If purpose can be found only in minds, then a universal purpose would have to be situated in a universal mind. A mechanical order would be that revealed in predictions based on calculable physical properties such as mass, velocity, and direction. But here too, since there appear to be events which are not purely material, such as human decisions, dreams, the fulfillment of human ambitions, and the like, the mechanist resorts to the *as-if* when he attempts to explain them.

Just as purposiveness is clearly a projection of a human trait into the nonhuman world, so is causality. By exerting effort, by making things, by interfering in the conduct of others, by preaching, by fighting for and against things, we have the impression that we are not entirely inefficacious. But few scientists are so naïve as to retain in their causal explanations the element of production. Most are willing to stop when they have formulated general statements of what happens when certain conditions are fulfilled. But this would not be done, were they not aware of the origin of the idea in human life and action.

They see the danger of anthropomorphism and are trying to avoid its consequences.

It is interesting to observe that when either of these metaphors is extended to cover all problems—that is, all of which the scientist is aware—the universal machine becomes purposive and the universal purpose becomes mechanical. For the very universality of purpose demands that everything contributing to its fulfillment act in a uform manner and that there be no wavering, no choice of means, no chance. The machines of which we know anything are built to act in precisely this way. Each of their parts is related to every other part so that the purpose for which the machine was contrived may be accomplished. The purpose is of course that of the inventor of the machine. But that is also true of the cosmic machine: its purpose is that of its Creator. On the other hand, when we are given a teleological universe in which the purpose is immanent, the fact that it is purposive is usually proved, as it was by Aristotle, by the demonstration that things, however diverse they may seem to be, always behave in a regular manner. If Nature were to build a house, says Aristotle, she would build it as a carpenter does. Technical rules become scientific laws, generalized descriptions as well as commands. Given then a single immanent purpose in the cosmos, it would be impossible to distinguish between its behavior and that of a machine.

Nevertheless the overtones of the two figures of speech are quite different. To think of the world as achieving a purpose, whether that purpose be clearly definable or not, is different from thinking of it as an enormous machine run by an unknowable engineer. Both concepts are swollen analogies. Neither is the more rational. Which metaphor will be chosen to name the cosmos is a matter of temperament. This appears very clearly in such questions as "What is it all about?" To say that it is about nothing, but is simply a system of interlocking cogs or, as the seventeenth century would have said, clockwork, would seem outrageous to the man who puts that kind of question. He may be satisfied with the awful spectacle of

universal law, as Seneca presumably was. He may find great
beauty in the regular order. He may decide that though he
cannot discover what it is all about, it is and must be about
something. Surely this is a common enough attitude to be accepted as typical of some minds. A more fundamental question would ask what justification we had for using such terms
as *The Cosmos, The Universe, The Whole.*

There is no answer to this question in which we can have
much confidence. Omitting for the time being just what is
meant by a whole, what kind of whole we are talking about,
the following answers occur to us. Men may have extended
their belief in the earth as the center of things to everything
which encompassed it. The notion of the earth as an absolute
center is early and plausible. After all one sees the sun and the
moon and some of the stellar bodies moving at least part way
round it. The fixed stars seem to stud a more inclusive group
of things and without a telescope there is nothing further to
be seen.[1] This picture as developed by Aristotle and his school
is the standard image of an enclosed universe forming a spatial
unit. The spatial relations of each item in this universe can be
more or less accurately defined and there is no evidence of anything else anywhere. Moreover, if it is assumed, as it was by
Aristotle, that it had no beginning and would have no end,
nothing needed to be posited as temporal frontiers. In view of
the special influence of Aristotle on Occidental thought, it is
probable that his *De caelo* was the literary, if not the psychological, source of the idea of *The Cosmos.*

In the second place, when religious beliefs in a Creator took
precedence over observation, and as far as we know they
always took precedence in the Occident, the limited universe,
that is, the earth and its surrounding bodies, had a definite beginning in time and in the minds of the Christian philosophers,
if not the Jewish, it would have an end. Thus it resembled a
living being which is born and dies. But as soon as people discovered that matter could not be created or destroyed, the

---

[1] Even with one we do not *see* what is further as further.

notion of the universe as having a beginning and an end lost some of its force. (Now, to be sure, such scientists as Hoyle are talking of the creation of matter presumably *ex nihilo*.) If something has a definite beginning and end, it can be thought of as a whole with longitudinal, if not lateral, termini. There is an anomalous feature in this argument which should be indicated. One of the firmest rules in Western thought has been that there must be a similarity between cause and effect. This was often employed critically to prove that the idea which we have of God as an infinite being could not have been fabricated by us who are finite. Why then was it not used in reverse to prove that God who is infinite could not have caused an effect which is finite?

But all this is conjecture and if people did think out their grounds for speaking of a universe, which is doubtful, those grounds would perhaps have been dialectical. There is probably a finite number of things in existence at any one time, and consequently philosophers could argue that they all have something in common which would be whatever it is which determines existence itself.[2] To take the simplest determinant, spatio-temporal location, it would be easy to argue that within the matrix of space and time this finite number of things exists and that the things form a network held together as the solar system or a drop of water is held together.

Let me repeat that I am not saying that this is the case or that a person saying so would be in an impregnable position. I am simply suggesting this as a possible point of view. If then a person could imagine the spatio-temporal matrix as something larger than the things which are in it, there would be

---

[2] I am assuming that this is a significant question, as it is when the existence of specific things is concerned. Thus one can significantly ask whether centaurs exist. But when "existence" becomes a universal predicate, like "being," then I fail to see why there should be any reason to ask what determines it. It is there and confronts us and that is the end of it. The trouble, like so many philosophic troubles, comes from our expanding the denotation of a common nontechnical term beyond its normal limits. The ancient rule, *Omnis determinatio est negatio,* could still be observed with profit.

obvious spatio-temporal boundaries to the cosmic collection. But even here, it should be observed, the notion of time which is not the duration of anything and of space which is not the dimensions of anything is a manifest figure of speech. The only times of which we have direct information are the times of the planetary revolutions, the time of the life cycle, the time beaten out by our pulse and respiration, the time of a moving body, and so on. These are to be sure usually correlated with astronomical or clock-time, but that is of no importance. Time as we know it is a measure of the changes which we know. A time in which nothing is happening whatsoever is like a space which encompasses nothing or is encompassed by nothing. None of this means that we cannot abstract the dimensions and erect them as a mathematical model, but that is far from saying that we have any evidence worth considering as a basis for a metaphysics in unoccupied space-time. We can imagine a railroad track continuing into infinity, but we do not believe that there exists such a railroad track. "Infinity" is a somewhat magical word and for that reason, if for no other, ought to be used with caution.

The Universe, The Whole, The Cosmos, I am saying, must, if the terms are to have an existential reference, refer to something which has boundaries. In short it must be thought of on the model of a thing, cut off from other things. The things which we are acquainted with have frontiers which are pretty unstable and they are established by whatever medium the things are set down in, on the crude level of common sense by the air or some other fluid. This is about as close as one can approach to the naïve style of thought. But along with the notion of things being cut off from other things is that of their internal organization: things hang together and do not fly apart. And when people speak of things, they sometimes emphasize their internal structure, sometimes their spatial limits. Living organisms, for instance, in spite of the give and take between them and the total environment, are usually thought of as structures which operate through the co-operation of their parts. And many an eloquent essay was written in the nineteenth century on the wonders of such co-operation by men who seem to have forgotten or to be ignorant of disease. The great example of such a structure was always the solar system, for the laws which described its inner relations were well known and easily understood. But no one had any evidence that the solar system was a pattern which could be inflated to cover all existence. Whether every star in the heavens is encircled by planets all moving about it as our planets move about the sun could be settled only by conjecture. It may have been a plausible conjecture, but that does not change its conjectural nature. We were simply extrapolating what we knew about one star to all stars and then maintaining that all solar systems had some theoretically definable relation to one another. That relation might have been purely spatial distances, gravitational or other dynamic relations, such that in some sense of the word each part of the supposed whole was dependent on every other part.

If the various sciences were so connected that the premises of one followed from the conclusions of another in one great deductive system, they would provide us with an intellectual model for a universe. But at present they are very loosely connected. No serious scientist would maintain that we know all that is to be known about even a single subject matter, let alone the logical interrelations of them all. We are quick to say that chemistry reduces to physics and physics to mathematics, or that biology is a physico-chemical discipline, but this reduction is more of a hope than an achievement. Having discovered chemical phenomena, we always have the possibility of discovering the physical conditions under which they occur; but given those conditions and no knowledge of chemistry, we would have no reason to deduce their possibility from purely physical theorems. Moreover, if we are in search of unity, the fact that one set of theorems is derivable from another in no sense of the word eliminates the differences in the facts expressed by the theorems. To argue that a certain dosage of whiskey is followed by a headache does not deny the reality of the headache; it states the conditions under which a headache will occur.

Again, to state the physico-chemical conditions under which alone life will appear does not permit one to say that there is no difference between living and nonliving matter. On the contrary, it is the observable differences which originate the problem of why it is found. If a living organism could be produced in a test tube, that would disprove the dogma of biogenesis. It would not imply that there was no difference between living and nonliving organisms, for if that difference did not exist, how would one know that one had produced a living organism in the test tube? Consequently, even if a unity of science were achieved, marvelous though it would be, it would not warrant our talking of the universe-as-a-whole. It would warrant talking of science-as-a-whole. The notion of *The Universe,* I am saying, is another basic metaphor.

Though the term has no discoverable denotation, it has a certain utility. For by thinking of all subject matters as somehow or other connected, we simplify our thinking and preserve an economy of ideas. The value of such economy has never been disputed though its significance has been misinterpreted. In one sense of the word the simplest account of things is a list of their proper names on the one extreme and on the other the most general adjective appropriate to them all as a collection. But since the traditional problem of the sciences has been to discover the interrelations of classes of things, whether that interrelation is causal, purposive, genetic, or even similarity of structure or substance, it is clear that the logical deducibility of one set of things from statements descriptive of another satisfies one of the principal conditions of a scientific explanation. It does not, however, simplify the things described in the sense of eliminating their radical differences. It is a simplification of knowledge, not of existence.

Alongside of the figures of speech which we have already mentioned, there are many others. Universal harmony, the strife of opposites, the reconciliation of antitheses, universal evolution both predictable and unpredictable, have been nuclei which have proliferated into systems. The development of the system from the nucleus is determined usually by inference supported by empirical evidence—at any rate the philosopher thinks it is. But the central vision or image or hypothesis (the name is unimportant) is not obtained by any logical process, except that of analogy. One may notice certain striking similarities between events of different orders, such as birth, growth, and death. The philosopher then hits upon the generalized picture of everything and the whole of things coming into being, growing, and dying.

He is immediately entangled in a mesh of problems. Things are usually born out of other things: out of what was the Universe born? This problem would not arise if the initial assumption had not been made that it must have been born out of something. But the assumption has been made and he is caught in a dialectical puzzle. If it was born out of nothing, then there is no explaining or understanding why it came into being. Its origin is a mystery. If it came into being out of something not itself, then the problem of the origin of things is simply pushed back a step. What has been called *The Universe* becomes only what has existed since a certain date in the remote past and either another name must be given to the Proto-Cosmos or it must be envisioned as simply a stage in the growth of the present cosmos. Neither solution is satisfactory.

Hence we land at a point at which we have to have recourse to myth, a more or less poetical version of an event which may never have occurred, but whose occurrence we are bound to think about because of our central image. Creation *ex nihilo* by a creator whose will, though beyond time, operates in time, gradually takes the place of a rational explanation. Rationally it might just as well be said that the world burst into being out of nothing as to say that it was created out of nothing, for neither sentence says anything which could be verified. But we are not here looking for verification of the scientific type. We want an image or a myth or a figure of speech which will do something for us which a scientific law can do only indirectly. But of this more later.

Such impasses are quite properly called ultimate since one cannot go beyond them. They represent the last words which reason can utter. If one says, as we have said, that they take on their peculiar sense because of the basic metaphor which is their foundation, that does not help us at all. For unless there is some way of thinking without analogies and figures of speech, we are bound sooner or later to reach an impasse. We can always stop wherever we please; that is undeniable. But we have no rule which can tell us when to stop and it is one of the peculiarities of the human mind that it will not stop until exhausted. We seem doomed to turn our pictures into representations, to turn metaphor into literality, failing as we do to understand that thinking itself is not copying the objective world but transforming it into a set of symbols. Any trope may become literal by use.

It is the general history of symbols to lose their symbolic meaning through attrition. Any dictionary will show that most of our words began as figures of speech. Omitting negatives and obversions, I find the following on a page of my dictionary: delicate, delicious, delict, deligation, delight, delineate, and so on. These happen to be Latin derivatives and their etymological meaning is therefore clearer than it would be if they came from Old English roots. Though the origin of our most ancient words is lost or is doubtful, there are some whose figurative meaning is still discoverable. Thus *buxom,* from O.E. *bugan,* to yield; *bower,* from O.E. *bur,* a chamber; *book,* from O.E. *boc,* which meant a beech tree as well as a book, because presumably the Teutons wrote on beechen boards. Only etymologists bother about the primitive meaning of such words; to the rest of us it is lost. But the loss of symbolic meaning is not restricted to words. It is probable that the cross was originally a symbol of the sun; that does not prove that the use of the cross in Christianity is a survival of a solar myth. In

Christianity it was, in the first instance, an instrument of torture and later acquired a new symbolic meaning. When it is used in jewelry or as an ornament, it is doubtful whether many people think of it as an instrument of torture. If they think about its meaning at all, it is a symbol of vicarious atonement. How much the average Christian knows about vicarious atonement is questionable. Even if he says "Christ died for our sins," he is likely to be ignorant of the implications of such a sentence, of the extension of the idea of the scapegoat, whether human or divine, of the accretions to the original idea which have arisen over the ages, of the differences between the Christian idea and the older Hebraic idea.

When we reach this point in our thoughts, we come upon a compact metaphor which does service for a whole complex of ideas. To explicate them all is no doubt impossible, but examples of such symbols are not hard to find. The letters of the alphabet were originally pictograms, as far as anyone knows, but who thinks of *A* as an ox or of *B* as a house? Nor does anyone think of the Alpha and Omega as an ox and a big O. Why the Phoenicians (or their predecessors) began their alphabet with the picture of an ox and ended it with a *T,* the pictorial significance of which has been lost, no one knows, nor does anyone know why the other letters of the alphabet were arranged in what has become our alphabetical order. Furthermore, this has become a matter of no importance. And yet we arrange ideas in alphabetical order, as if it were the most obvious of orders, when we make indexes or catalogues of books. What we want is an order which is established as a tradition and we no longer care what the origin of the order happened to be. Nothing is more amusing than the order of articles in an encyclopedia or of the words in a dictionary when one thinks of the logical connections between them. But since anyone using such books knows the alphabet by heart, he accepts the order as a guide. But the arrangement of the articles of an encyclopedia in alphabetical order is a modern device and it is clear that the alphabet was not invented to serve such a device.

The retention of old symbols to signify new meanings is normal. It is analogous to the retention of obsolete instruments and institutions and their metamorphosis into works of art. It gives men the illusion that they have defeated the passage of time and that above the flux there is permanence. As utility fades, beauty emerges, and instead of justifying our affection for certain things and practices by their instrumental value, we justify them as good-in-themselves. Anything may be good-in-itself and also useful, so that there is no telling ahead of time which kind of value is pre-eminent. History alone tells us that. If we know why an instrument was invented, we obviously know that it once had instrumental value. But that does not imply that it was not at least potentially an object of art. The fact that the dance was originally religious ritual or magic did not prevent its turning into something else, nor is there any reason why we should keep in mind its primordial historical purpose while watching the performance of a dance. A person who travels to the American Southwest to watch the Indians dance a corn-dance or a rain-dance may try to identify himself with the Indian dancers and to feel the emotions which he imagines that they feel. But others watch it as a spectacle. Outwardly both the Indian and the non-Indian spectators see the same thing. But the significance varies. This, however, is true of any work of art from exotic or early cultures. It is possible because in part whatever meaning a symbol has is contributed by the person who uses it. The religious paintings of the Middle Ages and early Renaissance were not painted to be hung in New York drawing rooms or in museums. But that does not prevent us from looking at them with intense emotion even when we are ignorant not only of their painters' intentions but also of the pictures' meanings. If this were not so, why would it be necessary for iconologists to write articles explaining their meanings?

No one knows how thinking began. We do not know why

men formed scientific theories, religious myths, and philosophic systems. Animals seem to get along pretty well without taking thought by following a routine even in matters of survival, migrations, storing of food, and raising families. If a savage really believed that a dance could bring needed rain, or that sticking thorns into dolls would kill his enemy, or that prayers to his gods with appropriate sacrifices would produce desiderata of other kinds, he would soon be disillusioned. For the very thought which was the source of such doings would also show him their futility. Savages are not fools and I am far from being the first to point out that in those matters which are immediately practical, like fishing and hunting, they are often more skillful than men of our own civilization. Their perceptions are often very acute, as is well known, their manual skill close to perfection. Furthermore, they had less precedent than we to go on. They too are a group of individuals of varying intelligence. And no doubt if an anthropologist should ask them why they continue to pray for rain since their prayers are so often inefficacious, they would reply as an American does when asked why he continues to pray for peace. A practice is not discontinued just because it is futile. It is continued for its own sake. We can always say that prayers for peace would bring results if we were worthy of peace, or that a drug would effect a cure if it had been given in time. But the replies are in answer to the wrong question.

We have a tendency to think that all human acts are done for an ulterior purpose which somehow or other can be inferred from the nature of the act. Thus we say that we eat in order to live, that we have sexual intercourse in order to have children, that we talk in order to communicate our ideas, that we save money against a rainy day, and that we punish criminals to discourage others from becoming criminals. But aside from the fallaciousness of such argumentation, we ought to have seen that, however instrumental an act may have been or could be, it is often performed with no thought whatsoever of its instrumentality. Savage societies would not have died out if they had not had to compete with civilized societies: those which have not been infected with civilization seem to survive. It is true that an Australian Bushman could not survive in Manhattan if he restricted his acts to those of his native culture. But that is beside the point. An insect cannot survive if sprayed with DDT.

There are, moreover, as far as I know, always reasons to be found for not surviving. We have adopted Horace's slogan on the sweetness of dying for one's country. The early Christians were delighted to die for their religion. Lucretia was willing to die to preserve her chastity. Men have killed themselves rather than face disgrace. The priests of Cybele castrated themselves to serve their goddess. Indian women lay down on the funeral pyres of their husbands. Japanese kamikaze pilots flew their planes into the ships which they wanted to sink and blew up with their bombs. When the *Titanic* sank, men stood aside and drowned so that women and children might be saved. Such incidents make one think that survival has been overplayed as a primary human motive. As a matter of fact, any act may take on a kind of sanctity, however absurd it may seem to people who have not sanctified it. All of which may throw some light on the mutation of symbols.

Any act which has become habitual becomes compulsive and therefore right. And the simple repetition of an act will make it habitual, no matter whether it has survival value or not. Attempts which used to be made by anthropologists to explain certain tribal customs, such as food taboos, as having a utilitarian value have all been shown to be futile. Eating one's totem or refusing to eat it or permitting only the priests to eat it on ceremonial occasions are customs which people who do not share them think of as nonsensical. They seem nonsensical since they may create hardship and do not bring about the results which outsiders think they ought to be expected to bring about. But outsiders do not see the real function of such customs and sometimes communal participation in an act is sufficient justification for performing it. Members of the tribe feel obligated to perform it and disgraced if they do not perform it. The degree to which an individual feels that he must participate in communal acts varies to be sure and in every society there are some recalcitrants. But nevertheless everyone feels some compulsion to do as others do, even when he sets himself up as the sole judge qualified to select what acts are to be shared.

In our own society the scholar accepts the methods, problems, and standards of his own social group and when he belongs to several such groups will easily switch his activities to conform as the group demands. The physicist who believes in the conservation of matter on weekdays will be perfectly able on Sundays to believe in transubstantiation. The clergyman who believes in the sanctity of life when the question of euthanasia is raised will nevertheless accept capital punishment of criminals. The philosopher who insists on the primacy of reason will nevertheless not ask what gives it primacy. All of us carry out certain rituals, not only in what we call our daily life but also in our special professions. For these rituals give stability to our behavior and assurance to our self-respect. How many laboratory scientists ever question or even analyze what they call the experimental method? How many philosophers ever question the application of the Law of Contradiction to existence? Such things are rules which must be followed under penalty of expulsion from the group. Diogenes the Cynic showed what would happen if everything was to be questioned, if a natural purpose was sought for every act and desire. He did not put the ultimate question as he crawled into his wine jar at night, which would have been the purpose of remaining alive.

There is no reason to look for the origins of thinking in its practical value. That it has practical value is true and we know enough about the history of thought to be able to say that sometimes a set of beliefs which seem to have no applicability to daily life turn out to be very useful. But the problems which trouble our curiosity may be purely intellectual problems such as an absence of consistency, a weakness of proof, dubious authority, badly performed experiments, *non sequiturs*. It consequently may well be true that some, if not all, people think for the sheer pleasure of thinking. And this is probably the truer, the farther one approaches to formal purity. For much thinking deals with the clarification of methods of thought which work well in ordinary affairs but are inelegant. To take but one example, we all use contrary-to-fact conditionals in our thinking, as when we say, "If I had not gone in swimming, I should not have caught cold," or, "If France had invaded the Rhineland as she was permitted to do by the Treaty of Locarno, Hitler would have been stopped in his tracks." Such arguments vary in their plausibility, but some are sound enough for all practical purposes. Thus a person usually follows the advice of a physician or lawyer or other type of engineer on the ground that such men know better what to do than we do. But what is such obedience to advice but assuming that if we do not follow it, things will not turn out as we wish? The logician, however, is hard put to it to formalize such reasoning and only a few years ago contrary-to-fact conditionals were ruled out of court by him.

We have a similar case of illogicality which works in some forms of experimentation. Sometimes an experiment is set up to prove an antecedent by affirming the consequent. For intance, it is suspected that a certain substance is present in a specimen under investigation. The specimen is given the usual tests and they come out right. It is then affirmed that the substance is present. But logically this is fallacious, for one cannot argue that if A is the cause of B and B is present, then A must have caused it, or that if P implies Q and Q is true, therefore P must be true. There are times when one knows in advance of the experiment that the only cause of B is A or that, as in definitions, implication happens to be a symmetrical relation. But such knowledge comes not from logic but from observation or, in the case of definitions, from fiat. The systematizing of scientific method has no practical value whatsoever, or at any rate none that is foreseen at present. For the conflict between existence and essence arises there as it always does when reason is applied to experience.

The closest approach which we have to a viable intellectual organization of experience is in statistics. For statistics recognizes the reality of particulars, variations within a class, patterns of change, and the probability, rather than the absolute truth, of one's conclusions. But statistics too has its rules and the rules cannot vary any more than the rules of formal logic can vary. They have been elaborated out of observations made upon the comportment of "large numbers" and of games of chance. They indicate to us the best bet which we can make on events. They have just as much predictive power as the rules of logic. The classes with which statisticians deal are not so purified as those of formal logic and the statistician is more tolerant of deviation than the logician, largely perhaps because he can calculate what the deviation may be expected to be. He is also closer to existence than the logician, since he can handle trends and is not forced into the reification of events. But as soon as he sets up, as he has to, a formal mathematical structure for his subject matter, he is in no better position than the logician is in. He envisions the world with a different eye, to be sure, and if he wrote metaphysics, it would be a quite different metaphysics from that of the Aristotelians. For to him an Aristotelian class would be simply a collection in which differentiation was imperceptible and the curve of distribution would shrivel to a point. But he is not usually a metaphysician and, oddly enough, no metaphysician has made a serious study of what a statistical universe would be like. C. S. Peirce and after him Josiah Royce did indeed regard statistics with some sympathy, but little of a metaphysical nature came out of their reflections on it.

Had they continued, they too would have had to have their basic metaphors. As they were in the process of deciding upon the nature of their ultimate facts, they would have had to find some name for events which would have differentiated them

from things or substances. To introduce a temporal dimension into things, they might have had recourse to biology and
spoken of growth and raised the metaphysical question of when
an event begins and when it ends. They would have had to
face the problem, as we have indicated above, of the lateral
frontiers of events and of that interaction between them which
tradition has called causal. They would have had to find new
phrases to describe cognition, for events cannot make an impact upon the end organs of the sensory nerves as things can.
This would have been very difficult to achieve for new metaphors gain acceptance very slowly. The attempt to invent some
can be seen very clearly in the work of Bergson with his *élan
vital,* his *énergie spirituelle,* his "intuition," his "vegetable
torpor," his "snowballs" and "sky-rockets," none of which did
more than capture the imagination of his readers for a decade
or two and then drop out of circulation. One of the difficulties
with new metaphors is that their metaphorical nature is too
clearly seen.

We easily forget that such a word as "cause" is a figure of
speech because it has been used long enough to become literal.
It was pointed out in the seventeenth century by Malebranche
that it names nothing observable and it was subjected to severe
criticism in the eighteenth by Hume and in the nineteenth by
Comte. But it is still in use, as we all know. The *élan vital* was
too obviously a figure of speech to be accepted generally and
yet no one has found a substitute for it. There are certain observable facts which neither what Bergson called the push
from behind nor the pull from in front will explain. The
growth of a seed into a specific plant may take place only in
certain special circumstances, but as soon as all the circumstances are put together, they are expressed in a restatement of
what takes place and not as an answer to the question of why
it takes place in that manner. It may be that the question itself
is illegitimate. It may be foolish to ask why insects, mollusks,
and vertebrates all develop eyes as distance receptors or why
some vegetables, insects, and vertebrates all form societies. Yet

there seems to be no common cause which operates in such cases and whatever common ancestor there may be for them all is so remote that we cannot resort to it for an answer. Moreover, whatever the ancestor of all three may have been, it did not have eyes nor was it social. And added to that is the apparent fact that some of its descendants did not develop eyes and others did not form societies. The *élan vital,* bursting out in all directions, now dropping off into something close to slumber, now vigorously pushing ahead in unpredictable ways, may not be an answer to the question, but it is an apt metaphor nevertheless for it is one which could be applied to a great variety of events though originating in one field alone.

It is ironical that the objection to the *élan vital* is made by men who do not object to mechanical causation. Suppose that we could state the conditions, which we cannot do, under which organisms would form societies and those under which they would not. Note that we cannot say, for instance, that those vegetables which became social survived and that those which remained solitary did not, for we actually find both the *compositae* and the *noncompositae* surviving. If we modify our statement to read, "The *compositae* survived because they formed a society," we are engaged in a tautology. Hence we resort to a description in general terms of what social organisms are and under what conditions they are found. But to say that these conditions determine the social organization of the organism is simply to substitute what sounds like a neutral word for the word "cause." If to cause something is a figure of speech, so is to determine something. The question then becomes which metaphor will be used.

Like Bergson after him, Peirce spoke in figurative terms when he wrote of natural law as the habits of things. He seized upon something which would both compactly name the regularity of natural events and permit diversity. But a habit when interpreted literally is the habit *of* something and Peirce does not seem to have provided a being which might develop the habits in question. If it is assumed that a great collection of diverse things began at some time or other to form habits which much later became laws, then the question still remains of why such diverse things should have formed the same habits. A survey of the field from minerals to men does of course show that each class of things permits general laws to be framed about its behavior. But to call them habits adds nothing to our understanding of the laws in question, if only because we have no cases on record when they did not have the habits nor any evidence of their actually forming them. Moreover, if we could go backward in time to the date when any class of things behaved in a very heterogeneous fashion, we should hardly be likely to call them a class at all. The word "heterogeneous" begs the question to be sure, but what other word could be used?

At the present time we are in a situation where the conclusions of the sciences, especially those of physics, demand new figures of speech from the philosopher. And the philosopher either throws up the sponge, turns the problem over to the poets, or says that the problem is meaningless. It is true that one cannot verify a figure of speech. We may feel its adequacy, but its nature is not such as to assert much of anything. To verify it would demand that it lose its metaphorical character. But if we could translate it into literality, we would not need it at all.

Before ending this section of our essay we may well raise the question of why certain metaphors become part of common speech and others not. To talk of the world as created is common, to talk of the world as everlasting is not. To talk of causes is common, to talk of ends is not. The English philosopher Collingwood with some justification spoke of three ideas which changed history: the Greek idea of nature as a living organism with a mind of its own; the Renaissance idea of nature as a machine with a machinist external to it; the modern idea of nature as a progressive evolutionary process. We can omit the question of attributing ideas to ages, but nevertheless can see that these three figures of speech have had wide acceptance.

The early Christian philosophers took over from the *Timaeus* the notion of God as a demiurge, but they eliminated from Plato's notion the factor of pre-existing matter which the demiurge would mold. The doctrine of creation *ex nihilo* became standard Christian doctrine. Plato's God was a sculptor, the Christian God a miracle-worker. Later on Aristotle's Unmoved Mover was given personality to such an extent that he could even feel love and was identified with the Biblical God. Yet all they originally had in common was their position in the order of things as what the French Revolutionists were to call the Supreme Being. The differences between what one might call the metaphysical God and the religious God were so great that one is hard put to it to imagine why anyone should ever have identified them. Yet they were identified.

Moreover, while Collingwood's notion of the Greek idea of nature as a living organism with a mind of its own was developing and gaining wider and wider acceptance, there existed and flourished another Greek idea which has proved more acceptable in our own times, namely, that of nature as a collection of tiny bits of matter moving exclusively in accordance with mechanical law. Though the atoms of Democritus were not identical with the atoms of Dalton, yet they were similar in their existing below the level of perception and in being mechanical, not teleological. This figure of speech also gained credence with one modification—the swerving of the atoms or, if one prefer, the introduction of chance—and in the philosophy of the Epicureans it was as widespread as any other basic idea. Can one seriously maintain that the triumph of the former metaphor in Christianity is attributable to the greater logical consistency of the theology which it phrased? Quite the contrary. Such questions cannot be answered with any hope of general agreement, but it surely looks as if the religious ideas had primacy and any philosophic theory which would justify them would have initially greater plausibility than one which would not. In Lucretius the Epicurean theory was antireligious, though far from atheistic, and it was much more difficult to accommodate it to the spirit of Christian theism than it was to accommodate either Plato's Demiurge or Aristotle's Unmoved Mover.

We do not feel ourselves to be able to posit any general rule establishing the development of such metaphors as Comte did, even if we admit that there is such a thing as "The Human Mind" which goes through stages of infancy, youth, and maturity. For (1) as Comte too saw, at any period there are always minds which think in the manner of earlier periods, and (2) a given man may be what Comte called theological in metaphysics, metaphysical in psychology, and positivistic in natural science. Yet in spite of these and similar reservations, it must be granted that more intellectuals during the seventeenth century thought in mechanistic terms than thought in organismic terms and that it was not until our own time that growth and other biological terms entered into philosophy.

Few if any people spoke of the dynamic, the creative, the vital in tones of praise before the middle of the nineteenth century, but now such adjectives are accepted by almost everyone as eulogistic. Is this because the material conditions of life are such that we feel a greater need for what is loosely called the creative than our great-grandfathers did? Is it possible that when craftsmanship was the rule, no one felt deprived of the love of making things and hence could look upon the machine with a kind of admiration and respect which we have come to reject? To this question I have no answer, but there is some evidence to make one believe that basic metaphors, often a projection of what men believe to be most characteristic of themselves, first satisfy an emotional need and second serve an explanatory purpose. If what is true of me is also true of the world as a whole, then I can understand the world as a whole. But this is all conjecture on my part.

It will be observed that common speech always contains residues from earlier periods. But one can find periods when two radically different ideas were equally common and yet one of them remained in circulation and the other did not. In seventeenth-century Great Britain both Neoplatonism and mechanistic causalism were equally popular. The number of intellectuals who followed Bacon, Hobbes, and Locke was, as far as I know, no greater than the number of those who followed Lord Herbert of Cherbury, Henry More, and Ralph Cudworth. In fact, Locke's *Essay* begins with an attack on the Neoplatonism of these men, an attack which would not have been necessary if they had not had an appreciable influence. The kind of Neoplatonism which they preached did not disappear, if it has disappeared, until the end of the eighteenth century. But it was sponsored by fewer and fewer men and finally, in such a writer as James Harris, came very close to lunacy.

Now it would not be fair to say that the triumph of what is badly called British Empiricism is attributable to its inherent reasonableness, to its harmony with common sense, to its settlement of ancient problems, to its high degree of internal consistency, to its support of traditional religious or political views, to the self-evidence of its first principles. It was in fact the source of more paradoxes than its rival. And it may well be that the public's desire to solve these paradoxes was one of the causes of its popularity. It also needed fewer and simpler assumptions than Neoplatonism. The picture of the mind as a piece of white paper on which impressions were made by objects in the world external to it, was surely as simple a figure of speech as could be found, whereas the picture of a mind out of which flowed theological, mathematical, logical, and moral truths was difficult to comprehend. It also may have appealed to the desire which many Englishmen had for intellectual egalitarianism. Moreover, since the rise from simple ideas of sensation to mathematical theorems was never completed, the more difficult problems of a sensationalistic epistemology were never faced.

Hence readers of Locke, Berkeley, and Hume were not so conscious of the tougher problems as the Neoplatonists were, for by the time they had mastered the more obvious, such as the subjectivity of sensory qualities, the existence of an external world, the reality of other minds, of the past, the future, and distant regions of space, they were exhausted and had no time left for the less obvious. That we had ideas which by their very nature could not have been impressed upon us by a material world was easily shown. And the descriptions of how they could have been compounded out of such impressions were hardly persuasive. Yet the doctrine in one form or another survived into our own time and not merely in naïve circles.

There is some probability that its harmony with the prevailing sciences accounted for much of its success. This was the great age of mechanical science. It was the period when physics progressed by freeing itself from teleological dynamics. The great names beginning about 1550 were Copernicus, Galileo, Kepler, Newton, and not Aldrovandi, Fabrizio, Severino, or even Harvey. Paracelsus, van Helmont, Aselli, and Bartholin all made contributions to biological science, but they are known only to historians of that subject. If their contributions had been made to astronomy or physics, the story might be different. We can see a similar situation in our own time. We are again living in an age when the prestige of physics is paramount. And when a physicist or astronomer speaks, we all drop our work and listen. This is not merely because some of these men have applied their knowledge to the destruction of the human race and that we feel terrified lest they wipe us all out. That may account for some of their prestige, for devils, witches, ogres, and maleficent giants have always captured the human imagination. But it has also usually been of interest to people to find out something about the more remote parts of the universe, even when the pressing problems of daily life are neglected.

The astrophysicist has pushed back the entrance to Heaven and the atomic physicist has opened the gates of Hell. One has the feeling of being suspended between two horrors, the nature of which can be understood only in the language of a secret society. The magician who resides in us all is inevitably seduced by the possibility of controlling horror. The Word which God spoke at Creation seems to many of us to have been translated into formulas which only the initiated can handle and the initiated are the nuclear physicists. And though we know that a common weed is just as marvelous as a solar system or an expanding universe, the ancient custom of locating the divine on high is too compelling to permit us to drop our eyes to the grass and the earth on which it grows.

It has been my contention in this chapter that all thinking is communicated in metaphors and similes and that declarative sentences lose their metaphorical character through use. In philosophical matters the metaphors are often derived from human behavior and are projections into the nonhuman world of acts and relations which only human beings can literally exemplify. But this is our way of understanding what goes on around us and, though people shift their analogies from time to time as their interests shift, they never reach the point of explaining any event in purely literal terms. A literal statement then is a statement whose metaphorical character has been forgotten.

4
Myth

THE PASSAGE FROM METAPHOR TO MYTH IS
very simple, for one has only to expand a metaphor into a
narrative and one has a myth. No one to be sure has ever done
this deliberately and consciously, as far as I know, though it
is possible that novelists and playwrights do something similar
when they take a central image or situation and then relate
what led up to it and what followed from it. We can imagine
Shakespeare as if he had never known anything about Geoffrey
of Monmouth's *The Chronicle History of King Leir* but nevertheless had thought of a situation in which a father is deceived
by the hypocritical expressions of love from two of his children
and the sincere simplicity of a third. Whether he gave away
his property to the former and disinherited the latter would be
of no importance. The dramatist would then decide how the
father would show the manner of his deception and what had
come of it. He need not have been a king; he could have
shown his gullibility in a variety of ways; the outcome could
have been comic as well as tragic. But all this presupposes a
Shakespeare who was not Shakespeare. For no writer writes in
a vacuum.

Shakespeare's imagination wandered about in a world already peopled by legendary figures, some of whom he had read
about, others of whom he had heard about. These legends gave
him, let us say, his start. But he also worked in a tradition in
which tragic figures were of the courtly class and comic of the

100

class of peasants, laborers, and rustic boors. Furthermore, from earliest Anglo-Saxon times one form of punishment was the confiscation of property, either in part, in the form of fines, or as a whole. Then too there were dozens of stories in which the youngest child, either boy or girl, was the most sincere, the most honest, the most intelligent, or the most ingenious. There was also the tradition which visited the sin of bastardy upon the bastard, so that for centuries a bastard could not even enter holy orders. We retain this feeling in the common use of the word for men of whom we intensely disapprove, sometimes deepening the intensity of our feelings by the interesting adjective "dirty." Finally, there was the long tradition of "The Wise Fool," allied to the sister tradition of "The Innocent Child." To imagine anything whatsoever depends upon having had some experience and a large part of experience is made up of our education. It would therefore be folly to exclude Shakespeare's reading and the stories which he had been told as a child, and indeed as a man, from his total experience. All this and his observation of men and women must have influenced his imagination. The story of his *King Lear* is the legend of *King Leir* as it was told by the chronicle play, rearranged as Shakespeare thought it proper to rearrange it and embellished with the marvelous poetry which he alone seems capable of writing. I am not using the word "embellish" here to suggest applied ornament, for I realize that, aside from the arias which Shakespearean characters occasionally sing, it is the poetry which gives significance to the ideas which usually are commonplace enough in themselves.

If now we think of the story as a myth, we notice at least the following characteristics. It is a narrative and it is also an emblem, in that it has what is sentimentally but truly called a "message." This message will be interpreted variously by different readers. There will be some readers who will be shocked by the mechanical balance of its development, the good Cordelia balanced by the evil Regan and Goneril; the good (legitimate) Edgar balanced by the bad (illegitimate)

Edmund; the deception by daughters of their father, by a son of another father; the fathers' failure to recognize the devotion on the one hand of a daughter and on the other of a son. In the very first scene there is a balance between the falsity of speech and the truth of silence. So it goes, establishing a seesaw pattern which is what, I suppose, aestheticians enamoured of form could call its aesthetic structure. To such people Shakespeare was trying to erect an emblem of Emerson's Law of Compensation and if the play came out unhappily, that is because in a world of perfect equilibrium there can no more be happiness than unhappiness. "An act is not wanted because it is good; it is good because it is wanted."

But suppose we are more interested in moral lessons than in aesthetic structures and patterns. Then we shall see in this play the ultimate triumph of the right against avarice, hypocrisy, and madness. The death of Cordelia will be interpreted as the King's punishment, not hers, and his madness will be the culmination of his initial weakness of judgment. Added to all this is the interaction of the Fool and the King which can also be thought of as the heart of the drama, for the paradox of wisdom's residence in the soul of jesters is one which has often captivated the attention of moralists. These are but samples of how this myth may be understood, how by accentuating one character or one scene and thus making it the core of the drama, one can switch the message of the play. It reminds one of a *passacaglia,* in which the bass remains constant and is overlaid with variations in the upper voices.

Now most of what I have suggested—and since I am not a critic my suggestions can be only rudimentary—could be said in a series of essays. If a man wishes to prove that good triumphs over evil; if he wishes to show that good and evil are always balanced; if he wishes to say that avarice is the dominant trait of some people, the *amor habendi* (love of possessions) conquering even filial affection, he may make a psychological analysis of a number of cases which would be perhaps much more convincing than a play. If he wishes to demonstrate the wisdom of the Fool, he may develop the theme of "cultural primitivism"[1] to the point that the only exemplar of "the natural," in one of its many senses, is the simple-minded man, the man who has retained a childlike heart and the child's supposedly clear vision of things. But when such thoughts are incorporated in a narrative, they take on a new dimension. In the first place, a mosaic of eternal ideas has been relocated in time. A set of general laws becomes a completely individuated history. A theoretical formula becomes infused with life. In the second place, no single thesis is expounded as it would be in a fable, but each reader is allowed to draw from the narrative whatever conclusion he wishes and none if he wishes none. Aesop's fables have each a single definite lesson which moreover is usually stated at the end. But *King Lear,* or any other drama of the sort, is so concrete that it is a sort of world of its own, self-enclosed and accepted as a specimen of nothing but itself. Just as we are confronted by people and forced to make our own interpretations of what they stand for, so we are confronted by the drama and similarly must try to make it intelligible.

I have spoken of *King Lear* as if it were a moralizing myth. In a way it is, for inevitably most people think of the moral lessons which can be learned from the lives of others. Such lessons need not be clear-cut at all, for one of the most profound moral lessons is the unintelligibility of human character. But we must not be drawn into that problem and shall return to mythography. Most of the myths which have occupied the minds of Western man are not simple moral lessons at all. There are creation myths, eschatological myths, aetiological myths, and myths, such as that of the dying and resurrected god, whose original meaning is lost. There are myths of culture heroes, of the origination of families, tribes, and nations, myths relating metamorphoses, such as those told by Ovid. Mythologists have classified myths and attempted to interpret them all

[1] For a discussion of cultural and other forms of primitivism, see A. O. Lovejoy and George Boas, *Primitivism in Antiquity* (Baltimore: The Johns Hopkins Press, 1935).

in accordance with one general principle, but their explanations are often as dubious, when they are supposed to be historical, as the literal meaning of the myths themselves. We no
more know why men make myths any more than we know why
they think or make comparisons. But we can, however, jot
down one or two observations upon myths.

Whatever else they may be, they are always concrete, or
what I have called historical rather than eternal. The men who
first told and believed the myths concerning Hera, Poseidon,
and Hephaistos surely did not think of their gods as simply the
names for Air, Water, and Fire. That came later when philosophers tried to "make sense" out of them. Similarly it was only
a century or so ago that Jews and Christians, faced with the
conclusions of the geologists, replaced the six days of creation
with geological epochs. Making sense out of something which
does not make sense is equivalent to translating the figurative
into literal speech and literal speech is scientific or philosophic
speech. Euhemerus transforming the gods into primitive beneficent kings, Philo transforming the three Patriarchs into the
three stages in the education of the Intelligence, the stages of
Instruction, Self-denial, and Grace, are both accepting a set of
facts which they believe to be well established and translating
legends into those facts. Philo believed that the education of
the Intelligence proceeded by three stages; he had the story
of the Patriarchs on his hands; he believed the story but felt
that as literal history it was improbable. He therefore turned
it into an allegory of which he had the key. Little is known of
Euhemerus, but it is possible that he too could not accept the
stories of the gods as literally true and hence, wishing to retain them in some form or other, interpreted them all as the
stories of culture heroes.

By the time of Clement of Alexandria, there were three
layers of meaning in certain stories: the literal, which he
called the imitative; the figurative, called by him the tropo-
logical; the allegorical or enigmatic. Thus the story of the
Deluge was literally true: at a given time there was a flood

covering the whole earth; it rained for forty days and nights; Noah and his family were saved, and so on. Tropologically it could mean the punishment of the wicked by the All-mighty and the salvation of the good. Enigmatically the Ark became the Church and the waters the waters of baptism. In later times the three layers became four, the fourth being the anagogical, through which one ascended to higher levels of insight. Such insight gave one religious truth, so that on the theory of four layers of meaning one had a single story which was literally or historically true, which stood for a moral principle, which was a symbol of an ecclesiastic rite, in turn a symbol on its own part, and finally the revelation of a religious truth.

It goes without saying that individuals differed in their interpretations of each myth or legend. In the Italian Renaissance, for instance, the story of Aphrodite and Ares, which was scandalous in Homer, could be interpreted as the union of Love and Strife, probably derived from the fragments of Empedocles as handed down by Diogenes Laertius. It gave one grounds for thinking of the cosmos as the marriage of conflicting forces, certainly an idea which must have been far from the intentions of Homer but which permitted a man like Leone Ebreo[2] to keep the story while purifying it. It is of no importance to us here what the correct or standard interpretation of the Biblical or pagan stories might be. What interests us is that men felt the need of interpreting them and that when they rewrote them as scientific and therefore literal interpretations of allegories, their need was satisfied.

It has often been remarked that primitive languages are more analytical than modern languages, that they have more distinctions in gender, tense, and even vocabulary. To call them analytical is a bit misleading, for that would seem to imply that the people who formed them first took certain of

[2] Leone Ebreo (ca. 1460–1535) was a Neo-Platonist born Judah Abarbanel. For a brief sketch of the philosophy of this interesting writer, see my *Dominant Themes of Modern Philosophy* (New York: Ronald Press, 1957), p. 66.

our concepts and broke them down, whereas they simply spoke as they saw fit and only later established a grammar. Be that as it may, even Homeric Greek, which is far from rudimentary, has three numbers in the verbs, singular, dual, and plural, and equally three voices, active, middle, and passive. Case endings are more complicated than ours and of course more attention is paid to the agreement between adjectives and what they modify. There are again more nouns in primitive languages for what we would call by one name. Whether this means that men used to think in more concrete terms than we do or not, I cannot pretend to say. For when one turns from speech to visual expression, the earliest drawings we have are all highly schematized: the cave paintings of animals are all in profile. Though it is erroneous to equate the "mind of primitive man" with the "mind of the child," we do notice that children when they begin to talk speak in proper nouns and then enlarge their denotation to cover all similar things. As Aristotle pointed out, children begin by calling all men "father."

The classification of similar things under a single rubric is something acquired, not a congenital trait. We have to learn to spot similarity; we do not possess the gift at birth. A child may call all men "father," but he does not confuse them with his own father. These gropings after groups and classes, which are the beginnings of science and the basis on which all scientific, as distinguished from historical, thought is constructed, are clearly made by us. Our earliest errors are errors in classification. The theory of the four elements, Earth, Water, Air, and Fire, in one form or another—for I am not referring only to the theory of Empedocles but to folk science—lasted until the end of the eighteenth century. Hence it must have seemed reasonable not merely to retarded minds but also to highly developed minds. It may be guessed, for there is no real evidence, that we begin our intellectual life with the apprehension of things, located here and now, and not with ideas in the sense of class concepts.

The myth is a return to the concrete or, if one prefer, a

retention of mental innocence. Divested of its concrete or existential language, it turns into scientific law, for only when the
concrete elements in myth are eliminated, can it be verified.
One cannot, for instance, directly corroborate a creation myth
for the obvious reason that the event which it narrates occurred centuries ago. But if the idea of creation is retained,
after purgation of the idea of a Creator, then one can investi-
gate both the possibility and the actuality of creation. When
Hoyle speaks of the creation of matter—presumably hydrogen
—in interstellar space, the word "creation" can mean only that
amounts of hydrogen appear in such places and that no antecedent cause or condition or determinant of its appearance can
be discovered. This may be simply a confession of ignorance.
But strictly speaking, it is the assertion of the appearance of
matter *ex nihilo*. It is assumed that one can actually discover
the matter which appears in this manner and that it is theoretically impossible to discover why it appears. This is surely
creation without a Creator and the emotional aura of the
creation story in Genesis is lost. But enough of it is retained
to induce its narrator to use a term to name the event which
has Biblical associations. In the nineteenth century such a
scientist would probably have said, "God—or the Supreme
Being or the Creator—creates matter at such and such times
in such and such places." But since the myth has been thinned
and purged of its religious implications, it seems better to say
that matter is created and nothing more.

In a case of this sort the return to myth as the concrete suggests, if it does not prove, the possibility of retaining traditional
modes of thought while being scientific at the same time. No
new myth need be invented to tell us how and why and when
matter is created nor by whom. For we have in the back of our
minds the first two chapters of Genesis. To say simply that such
and such matter appears, or even to state the conditions under
which it appears, would not have the same associations. And
if we did not remember the opening of Genesis, the word
"creation" would be as opaque as any other word. The use of

the word does not commit us to any particular theology; in fact, by itself it commits us to nothing more than a denial of the principle *ex nihilo nihil*. But regardless of that, the connotations of creation can be overlooked and the only criticism of the usage would probably come from scientists who felt those connotations strongly enough to object.

We have already said that the use of a cause to explain events is the residue of a metaphor, a metaphor which is itself the residue of a myth. Whatever philosophers may have said in criticism of causalism, most of us retain some sense of the cause's producing the effect, much as an artisan produces the objects of his craft. Mixed with this is the metaphor of birth: the effect must proceed out of the cause. Hence there must pre-exist in the cause enough of the effect to justify the slogan *ex nihilo*. This in turn has given rise to the conclusion that whatsoever traits of the world cannot be equated or identified with pre-existent traits belong to "appearance," not to "reality." And since the only trait which could be so equated was mass, ponderable matter became the one reality. By this time nothing was left of the original myth as far as scientific reasoning was concerned. For each event one had an equation. Everything which was actually produced was swept away as appearance. This gave rise to a new picture of the world, a picture in which there was a foundation of undifferentiated matter, bits of which moved about at varying velocities, above that the sensory appearances called colors, sounds, tastes, and the like, and above (or at least different from) that the private world of the individual, his feelings, dreams, and illusions. The only causal efficacy remaining was in the bits of matter, in spite of certain obvious facts such as men being terrified by hallucinations, depressed by dreams, or working hard to obtain certain sensory impressions. When one tried to form an image of causal efficacy, the image was that of billiard balls bumping into one another and rebounding. But since matter had the power of presumably producing by its clickings and bumpings the whole range of sensory impressions with all their richness and variety, and moreover the power of producing them *ex nihilo,* matter became invested with some of the creative magic of God. Here was a myth in germ which required only a poetic imagination to develop it. But somehow or other the materialists either lacked that kind of imagination, or, if they did not, were ashamed of it and at most attributed to something called nature what they should have attributed to matter.

Contrasted with the metaphor of a cause is that of a purpose. And this too seems to be the residue of a myth. As we pointed out above, the only purposes of which we have direct acquaintance are our own. We know that we do things to achieve given ends and we project into the lives of the higher animals, which we naturally think of as not too different from our own, purposes analogous to ours. We say that the birds build their nests, the spiders spin their webs, the bees organize their hives, for purposes which would be ours if we did such things. The determination of the purpose is the end which these artifacts actually serve. But in this case we do not say that the animals know what ends they are aiming at; we are more likely to speak of the purpose as inherent in the activity. So we say that the heart exists in order to pump blood through the body, the lungs to provide oxygen, the ears to hear, and the eyes to see. It is no longer our purposes which are under discussion but those either of the organs themselves or of the God who created them. If we are going to see, then we need eyes, and if we are going to hear, we need ears. The analogy here is to the tool or instrument made to do one thing and one thing alone. But it will be observed that the purposes of such instruments are different from the purposes which a human being as a whole might have. In the latter case we are freer of specified tools and we prove our purposiveness by thinking up a variety of ways in which to attain them. We want something and we try out one way of getting it, usually the way to which we are accustomed.[3] If that way does not work, or is blocked by an

---

[3] Many of our more complicated machines begin by resembling the machines which they are replacing. The first attempts at aeronautics

unforeseen obstacle, we then have to think up some new way of getting round the block. If the eyes go blind, we substitute our fingertips when we want to read. And when our ears get weak, we supplement them with hearing aids. But the obsolete machine or the atrophied organ can do nothing for and by themselves, nor can the spider apparently find a substitute for its web or the bird for its nest.

The ultimate projection of purpose beyond human life is that proposed by a philosopher like Aristotle, who finds no explanation of a change satisfactory until he has discovered its purpose. There is no need of another exposition of his teleological physics, for it is well known, but it may be worth pointing out that when he says that a body moves in order to regain its natural position, or that an egg develops in order to produce a chicken, he discovers the purpose by observing the most frequent termination of the processes and calling that their purpose. But to do this, he has to think of the world as it would behave if no human beings were in it. For human beings have the unhappy faculty of disturbing the regularity of nature, removing stones from their natural position, bringing fire down to earth, eating seeds and fruit before they can grow into flowers and trees, preventing young animals from reaching maturity, and using wood to build houses. If we were not around, presumably all nature would pursue an orderly and uninterrupted course, except where chance interferes. So that the natural order in Aristotle, though frequently called "that which happens on the whole," is that which would happen on the whole if the regular order were not broken. In that event all processes would inevitably attain their determinate goals and those goals would be the purposes of nature. Purpose thus becomes simply the name for the regular sequence of events

---

were made by means of artificial wings. If a boat is rowed, power is first attached to oars. If a carriage is pulled by a horse, the automatic carriage will look like a horse-drawn carriage. Men's coats still have vestigial buttons on the cuffs which button nothing. Electric lamps still, though not always, are set on bases which are jars formerly used to hold oil.

and, except for the emotional flavor of the term, could be exchanged for "natural law."

If we could imagine a philosopher setting out to build a philosophy without previous reading of the masters of his subject, we might think of him as confronted by two sets of events, those which are orderly and constant in their order, and those which are disorderly or fortuitous. The question immediately arises of which set will acquire a eulogistic name. For when we attach the name "Nature" to a set of facts, we usually think, if we may rely on the history of the idea, that it confers greater value to the facts than such a word as "disorder" or "chaos." Certainly our everyday experience shows us more variety than unity, more randomness than perceptible order, more change than permanence and, if we were to rely on such experience for evidence of what the world is like, we should conclude that order is rarer than disorder, permanence rarer than change. This has always been recognized by some philosophers who have distinguished between *The Flux,* the world of perception, and *The Law,* the world of reason. To endow something with a eulogistic name can mean only that we think highly of it. That is obvious. Hence we may conclude that the human mind thinks more highly of the orderly than of the disorderly, of the permanent than of the mutable, of the unified than of the diverse. This being so, the discovery of a scientific law is not emotionally neutral; it is a good. And when we find our search for the good satisfied or nearly satisfied, we say that we have attained or are on the road to attaining our ideal.

Hence the emotional flavor of such a phrase as "the purposes of nature" is important. For it provides us with a link between science and religion. It allows men to ask, "Why are we here?" or, "What is the meaning of it all?" The answer to the question "Why?" is not some antecedent cause at all, but a purpose. One cannot, that is, reply to the first question, "Because one of several million spermatozoa happened by chance to penetrate an ovum." The answer to the second question must be a moral answer, but the purpose and the value involved cannot be ours, for we did not exist when the process ending in our presence here on earth was started. They are therefore attributed to some power, capable of having purposes and establishing meanings, which is greater than ourselves and pre-existing our existence. This power, which is inevitably anthropomorphic, is what is usually called God. But once this point is reached, new problems arise. Some good must be demonstrated in the cycle of birth and death, the struggles of men against the hostile forces of wind, rain, floods, earthquakes, and avalanches, as well as in the apparent injustice of personal misfortune.

There would be no sense in talking about the problem of evil unless there were some reason to believe that all things ought to be good. We no longer would ask what good is achieved by white light passing through a prism and breaking up into the seven spectral colors, or why we do not have four legs instead of two, or why we breathe oxygen instead of nitrogen. Such questions have been asked in the past but we are likely to accept them when discussed in a purely scientific context as hard facts which we must accept as the basis of our philosophizing. But in a teleological context every hard fact should be expected to serve some good or to aid in serving some good. The myth not merely of a Creator, but of a purposive Creator, remains when such questions are put and moreover the purposive Creator is supposed to have only beneficent purposes. But since sometimes we cannot with all the good will in the world discover what they are, we are driven to the conclusion that the Will of God is beyond understanding and that we must either rebel against it, which would be futile, or resign ourselves to its acceptance. But if God's purposes are inscrutable, they might just as well be simple unpurposive facts, as far as science is concerned. But, it will be replied with some justice, science is not enough concerned with what matters most to men.

Kant's *Critique of Practical Reason* is based on the premise that science cannot give us any justification for living a moral life and for believing that we have duties to perform. Physics, chemistry, and biology are rational disciplines, it is said, which handle facts, not values. Consequently if we have no knowledge other than rational, we have no grounds for ethics. The physicist cannot prove, and is not interested in proving, that it is better for the speed of light to be an ultimate velocity or that the atomic theory is morally edifying. The chemist does not pretend to say that we can derive a set of moral laws from the constitution of matter, and when the biologist speaks of the survival of the fittest, he surely does not use that superlative to mean the best. These are not of course Kant's examples. Now he might have concluded that there is no justification for ethics since science tells the whole truth about life and the stage on which it is lived. But on the contrary he concluded that we have the right to believe in what is essential for morality, in his eyes the existence of God, the freedom of the will, and the immortality of the soul.

We shall not debate the question of whether or not these three beliefs are essential to morality but confine ourselves to his reasoning. That is grounded upon the premise that the universe is so built that we can live a moral life in it, as he conceives morality. He does not question this. He does not say, "Perhaps we cannot be moral; perhaps our standards of good and evil, our sense of duty, are man-made and have no further justification." On the contrary, he has the belief that such an ethics would have no binding force on men and that the world as described by science is amoral and gives us the freedom to behave in any way we please, regardless of the pleasure or pain or other apparent goods and evils which might exist in it.

Instead of trying to base value on fact, Kant does the reverse, and gives us the possibility of holding to factual beliefs based on our beliefs about value. The myth of a moral God, whose commands are not merely natural law but also moral law, takes precedence over the conclusions of science. Every man does have a sense of right and wrong, though many men disagree with one another over what is right and what is wrong. It is also true that we can discover the social origin of many of our standards. For though all men as biological specimens have the same appetites and "drives," no society allows its members to satisfy them in any way they please. There is more latitude in some than in others and what is praised in some is reprehended in others. Moreover, there is always a certain amount of recalcitrancy in every society, some members always refusing to obey the general laws and customs. It may be possible to correlate, for all I know, the kinds of sanctions which are applied in any society with the organization and environment of that society: the way in which its members earn their living, the climate in which they live, the threats which their environment presents to them, the size, stability, and composition of the population. I doubt that any such correlation has been made in any detail, but that is beside the point. Even if it were made, the criticism would be voiced that social sanctions are not enough, unless it can also be proved that they express or are harmonious with the commands of a moral order. What a number of ethicists want is some ground for believing that some acts are good or evil regardless of what any individual or social group commands. Otherwise, it has been said, we have no right to condemn Hitler for his mass executions, for the Nuremberg Laws, for the concentration camps, and for his war-making. The most we could say would be that we do not like Nazi customs.

It is not my intention to argue this point at length, but it should be said that the evil of Nazism appears only when one thinks of the whole human race as the society to which it might apply. Nazism was approved of by 44 per cent of the German voters in their last free election and if there had been only Germans in the world, no one would ever have discovered that it was an evil system except its victims. And they were prejudiced. To call any local set of customs evil is to imagine it as extended way beyond its local frontiers, and it is questionable whether that is good logical technique. What actually was being done by the critics of Hitler was to apply their standards to Germany as if Germany were then part of their own cultures. They were also struggling to universalize ethical standards, not by basing them upon human nature in general, which would be impossible since all men live and have to live in some sort of society, but by universalizing human nature on the model of the Christian Occident.

The theory of standards known as cultural relativism does not collapse simply because we want universal and absolute standards. When people obey a law, it may be from a variety of motives. It may be, for instance, from fear of punishment, should they violate it, from a decision that laws legally passed should be obeyed regardless of what one thinks of their wisdom, from a conviction that the governments we have are given us by God, from downright agreement that the laws are right and just. We have in modern Western society at least two sets of law, those derivative from the Bible, as we understand it, and those of the state. As far as I know these are not in conflict where there is a possibility of conflict. The conflict does not exist in the case of the Commandments against polytheism, swearing, and honoring one's parents, though it would probably arise if one were to set up a polytheistic religion including devil worship, or if one were to swear and curse in public to the serious annoyance of others, or if one were to dishonor one's parents in some manner proscribed by statute. But in some states Sabbath-breaking is prohibited. In all states theft, adultery, murder, and false witness are crimes and not merely moral misdemeanors. Now a thief may know that he is breaking both a secular and a divine command, and yet commit theft. An adulterer may believe neither in God nor in the sanctity of statute law. A murderer may not believe in God and yet know that murder is a crime. So that the authority behind our standards of right and wrong is far from omnipotent. It can be and frequently is defied. A psychiatrist might be able to determine why people break the law, but I doubt that all psychiatrists are agreed upon it. My point is simply that the knowledge of a moral standard's having been established by supernatural authority gives it no more efficacy as a deterrent than the knowledge that it is established by majority vote.

Moreover, many customs known to rest only on tradition and to be of little rational importance are carried out with great fidelity. Men and women will obey certain demands of social etiquette much more strictly than they obey the Ten Commandments. Civility, good manners, and proper speech may seem like trivial matters, and yet they obtain much more general respect than what the books call the fundamental ethical principles. The only penalty for being rude, ill-mannered, and slovenly in speech is social disapproval, the disapproval, moreover, only of that particular social group with which one is identified. And yet that suffices to keep most people in line. No one actually thinks, when he thinks, that there is anything divine in courtesy or in the correct pronunciation of words; no one to the best of my knowledge thinks of such matters as anything more than "what is done." But I venture to say that such rules and regulations are treated more seriously than such moral principles as the prohibition of lying. One cannot, if I am right, maintain that supernatural sanctions alone will regulate morals and establish effective standards of good and evil. Such sanctions are no more effective than regard for one's reputation, and since their application is usually believed to be deferred until after death, it is only to be expected that they should be less powerful than the sanctions which come into play here on earth.

Yet it will be noticed that in criticizing this belief I have made use of the very myth on which it is based. I have used it to be sure in residual form. Instead of saying that God, the Creator and Judge, inflicts punishments or rewards during life or postpones them until after death or on the Day of Judgment, I substitute for God the State or Society or the Law or the Government or some other equally mythical being, which acts as if it were empowered to express the will of God. If people were to believe that the State is just a group of individuals and has no unity of substance, nothing correspond-

ing to the soul or person, it is doubtful whether most of them
would pay much attention to its commands. For we cannot
discuss morals without introducing commands or standards,
and it is impossible or so it seems, to think of a command
which is not commanded by a person or quasi-person, of a
standard which is not extra-individual.

Many of us have reached the point which Antigone reached,
which the Christian martyrs reached, and which all conscien-
tious objectors reach, where the conflict between what the
individual believes to be right and what civil authority says is
right demands a solution. No compromise is possible here for
one has to choose between two irreconcilable imperatives. If
a man believes that it is not right to kill other men and the
state orders him to do so, he can no more reconcile the opposition than he can move eastward and westward from the same
point at the same time. He has to choose. There is, it would
appear, no rational way of deciding the issue and men have
been willing to die rather than violate what they believed to be
right. There have been philosophers, like Hegel and his school,
who have insisted that the state is a person and that the individual's will must be made harmonious with that person's
will. This is in direct conflict with the teachings of the Catholic
Church as expressed by Leo XIII. In the Encyclical, *Quod
Apostolici Muneris* (December 28, 1878) we find that Pope
saying,

> Assuredly, the Church wisely inculcates the apostolic
> precept on the mass of men: "There is no power but
> from God; and those that are, are ordained of God.
> Therefore he that resisteth the power resisteth the
> ordinance of God. And they that resist purchase to
> themselves damnation." . . . And if at any time it
> happen that the power of the State is rashly and tyran-
> nically wielded by princes, the teaching of the Catholic
> Church does not allow an insurrection on private
> authority against them, lest public order be only the
> more disturbed, and lest society take greater hurt there-

from. And when affairs come to such a pass that there is no other hope of safety, she teaches that relief may be hastened by the merits of Christian patience and by earnest prayers to God. But, if the will of legislators and princes shall have sanctioned or commanded anything repugnant to the divine or natural law, the dignity and duty of the Christian name, as well as the judgment of the Apostle, urge that "God is to be obeyed rather than man."[4]

The one thing omitted from this passage is an indication of how one knows when the legislators and princes have sanctioned or commanded anything repugnant to the divine or natural law. But fortunately for Catholics, there is always a confessor or spiritual adviser at hand to produce the necessary information. At any rate the doctrine is clear as far as our present interests are concerned. And the whole Encyclical, as well as others issued from the pen of Leo XIII, insists that legislation must be harmonious with divine law while also maintaining that the state exists if not, in the words of another Pope, *ad nutum et patientiam Ecclesiae,* at least *ad nutum et patientiam Dei.* The factor which is relevant to our present discussion is that the myth of the state as a person is retained, thought of as having power, giving commands, and being moral and immoral. The probable justification for this myth is the historical fact that sovereignty has at times been vested in individual human beings, princes, who could of course be all these things and more. But when personal sovereignty is exchanged for collective sovereignty, we attribute to the latter all the traits of the former, excepting usually the less desirable traits.

A clearer case of a myth in this context is that of the social compact. The originators of this story knew that it was not historically true; none of them, so far as I know, really believed

<hr/>

[4] See *The Church Speaks to the Modern World,* edited and annotated and with an Introduction by Etienne Gilson (Garden City, N.Y.: Doubleday, 1954 [Image Books]), pp. 193 f.

that at a given date people came together and decided either
to surrender their personal sovereignty to a monarch, as in
Hobbes, or to band together for protection, as in Rousseau.
But if one assumed that men were "born free," regardless of
whether one thought their freedom a source of nasty brutish-
ness, as Hobbes did, or of timidity and helplessness, as Rousseau did, then some explanation was needed for their present
lack of freedom. It was also assumed that their lack of freedom
must be made to seem desirable. They must be shown to have
gained more than they lost.

The myth of the social compact was useful in performing
both of these tasks, for none of the philosophers who used it
denied that man in society is restrained from doing certain
things that he might want to do and the two whom we have
mentioned also believed that the present condition of man was
better than his condition before the compact was agreed to. It
was essentially an exercise in apologetics and all the more
curious in that there was no evidence whatsoever that men had
ever been free in the sense of being asocial. But in order to
remedy the evils in a system, one has the feeling that one
should know their cause and in social matters the easiest way
to discover it was to assume a fall from a better state, for that
was harmonious with the dominant tradition. In Christianity
the fall was of course due to original sin; in pagan philosophers
it was ascribed to various things: to the apparently inevitable
degeneration of everything which lives in time, to the institution
of private property, to the *amor habendi,* even to international
trade.

But to those philosophers whom we are mentioning at
present, those who utilized the myth of the social compact, the
present state was not necessarily worse than man's original
condition. To Hobbes, for instance, absolute monarchy, which
had preceded the Revolution, was the best of systems, limited
only by what he called the Laws of Nature. The social compact, while changing an original condition in which all men
were free, did not change it for the worse but for the better.

And though its proponents might not think it the best of all ideal conditions, they did think it was the best possible arrangement. For even Rousseau insisted that the common will was always right. In view of the outcome of their thinking, one can legitimately ask what service the myth provided.

Here, as so often in discussions of this type, one can only guess. All myths are fictions or, if one prefer, symbols made by man. They point to a way of thinking, not to facts which have been discovered. And the way indicated by the myth in question is that of thinking in terms of individual human beings with desires which are reasonable and are then fulfilled. Though the psychology of volition was probably wrong, in that people do not usually formulate their desires in accordance with preliminary planning, tradition held the contrary. One first saw what was good and then did it. To imagine the primitive men of Hobbes, accustomed to a "nasty, brutish, and short" life, becoming dissatisfied with it and then gathering, one supposes, round a council fire and agreeing to exchange their freedom for security, is almost impossible. For not only do most men cling to the habitual as sacred, but in a world in which the war of all against all is the custom, victory would have determined the right.

In Locke the shift from the original condition is even more bizarre, for if the primordial sovereignty of the people is retained while effective sovereignty is exercised by a limited monarch, one wonders again why the people should ever have agreed to sacrifice any part of their power even to an agent of their desires. For one visualizes the horde of freemen as simply taking what they wanted and relying on their individual muscles to keep it. This would have been intolerable to Locke, but there is no evidence that it would have been intolerable to the presocial savages. The same observation applies to Rousseau's myth. His simple pastoral people, whom he describes as being pretty close to the ideal, would have had no reason to agree on abandoning their peaceful existence. And whatever the misfortunes of such an anarchic life might have been, they too would in all probability have accepted them as the will of their gods. But all three philosophers seem to have projected their own personalities into the parties to the contract, as if they were saying, "If I had lived in this manner, I would have preferred something else and would have assembled with my neighbors, who would of course have been like me, to form a more perfect union." If my guess is right, then what they did was to find intellectual solace in explaining something not by the pressure of material or natural forces, but rather by the fulfillment of a human desire. Just as the universe had to be created and moreover created by an anthropomorphic god, so society had to be created and be created by an anthropomorphic People.

The solace lies in the humanizing of one's facts. The facts have to be envisioned as something made or destroyed, loved or hated, improved or deteriorated by anthropomorphic beings. The ancient myths arose we know not how, but such myths as that of the social compact or the economic man or the state or the people, were invented in historical times and in some instances with full knowledge that they were myths and not historical incidents. But just as the modern Christian finds the world more of a home if he can believe that it is under the governance of a beneficent God, so the social scientist finds social problems more intelligible if he can interpret them as arising in the life of a semi-divine individual. One cannot run the risk of saying that every Greek believed in the existence of the goddess Demeter who made the grain grow, whose daughter was abducted by the god of the underworld and kept below for four months of the year and permitted to emerge for another eight months. But even the sophisticated Greeks repeated the story, just as sophisticated Christians repeat the story of the six days of Creation, the Tower of Babel, the Deluge, the Ten Plagues of Egypt, and so on. Rather than abandon the myths, both pagan and Christian, we allegorize them in order to keep them in acceptable form.

But the question must be raised of why one bothers to allegorize them. One does not allegorize the atomic theory of Democritus, the theory of the four elements of Empedocles, the Great Animal and the eternal recurrence of the Stoics. One makes no special effort to reinterpret the theory of the four humors or of astral influences so that they will fit in with contemporary science, even if we do still speak of sanguine, melancholy, choleric, and phlegmatic people or of jovial, martial, and saturnine people. In short, I am suggesting that an explanation which stops short of myth will seem incomplete, and the myth which will complete it must humanize the events which are being explained. If this hypothesis is correct, then we can see why teleological explanations hang on in areas where they are scientifically superfluous and why, when a scientific law is well established, men will still raise the question of its meaning for human life.

Note that it is the meaning of the theory, not of the facts. For presumably the facts do not change when a new explanation of them is given. But though bodies fell with a constant acceleration of about 32 feet per second before Galileo and planets revolved about the sun directly as the product of their masses and inversely as the squares of their distance, these facts had no meaning until they were expressed in formulas and integrated into common beliefs. The word "meaning" in this context does not mean denotation. People who use it are not referring to the facts which are supposedly generalized in the law. They are usually referring, on the contrary, to the emotional effect of the law if one believes in it, or to its effect upon one's religious or moral beliefs. Since the word "meaning" is so hopelessly ambiguous, it would be useful to find some other word for it when it is used in this manner. I shall therefore adopt the less precise term, "significance," to name both the denotation of a word or sentence and its emotional aura. The myth, I am now saying, preserves the significance of the facts stated in any law or scientific theory. Scientific statements are supposed to be free from all significance and one's feelings about them or their supposed implications are irrelevant to their truth. Yet if the theory of organic evolution, for instance, has an emotional aura and also implications for morality and religion, then we cannot expect human beings, when they are not doing biology, to be insensitive to them.

No historian of ideas forgets how the intellectual world reacted to the publication of *The Origin of Species* and *The Descent of Man*. The inferences which were drawn from these books were often contradictory, some optimistic, some pessimistic, some harmonious with traditional Christianity, some discordant with it, some promoting social, economic, and hygienic reforms, some deprecatory of them. Progress both from bad to good and from "lower" to "higher" were inferred from the struggle for existence and the survival of the fittest. Some saw the hand of a directing God in the evolution, for instance, of the eye from a sensitive pigment spot to the complicated human or avian eye. Others saw it all as what they contemptuously called blind chance, as if determinism was less blind than chance. Some writers, like Flinders Petrie, argued that hospitals, both mental and physical, were a waste of time and futile opposition to one of Nature's laws. Some, like Kropotkin, argued that mutual aid was as natural as warfare. Before 1859 Spencer had generalized the concept of evolution to extend it to all change, whereas Wallace and Darwin were exclusively interested in the history of speciation. There was not a human interest which was unaffected by belief and disbelief in the theory, whether in its narrow or extended form. On the emotional side there was consequently both elation and depression, and whether men were influenced in the inferences which they drew because of their emotions or were stirred emotionally by those inferences, I shall not attempt to say, for significance cannot be analyzed into two existentially different aspects. The emotional and the logical were cemented together.

The mythical nature of all this appears in the various ways in which Evolution with an initial capital was used. The best, if the most trite, example is the verse, "Some call it Evolution, others call it God," which was historically accurate if poetically inept. The word denoted merely a genetic relationship between the various forms of living beings. It was only derivatively a substantive. But it did not take long for it to turn into one and to become capable of doing things. It could be relied on to produce better and better effects. It should not be opposed, but allowed to run its course. Its *modus operandi*—and here one overlooked the fact that it was itself a *modus operandi* and not something which had one—was a model for human beings to copy. In short, it was personified. The conclusion of "In Memoriam" is the standard example of this transformation of a scientific theory into a myth, when it speaks of "a soul" which "strikes his being into bounds,"

> And, moved thro' life of lower phase,
>   Result in man, be born and think,
>   And act and love, a closer link
> Betwixt us and the crowning race
>
> Of those that, eye to eye, shall look
>   On knowledge; under whose command
>   Is Earth and Earth's, and in their hand
> Is Nature like an open book;
>
> No longer half-akin to brute,
>   For all we thought and loved and did,
>   And hoped, and suffer'd, is but seed
> Of what in them is flower and fruit;
>
> Whereof the man that with me trod
>   This planet was a noble type
>   Appearing ere the times were ripe,
> That friend of mine who lives in God,
>
> That God, which ever lives and loves,
>   One God, one law, one element,
>   And one far-off divine event,
> To which the whole creation moves.

It is true that "In Memoriam" was first published nine years before the appearance of *The Origin of Species*, but, as has been recently shown,[5] evolutionism as a general mode of explanation, and indeed all the data which Darwin brought together to substantiate his special doctrine, were in circulation well before 1859. There was nothing in any of the strictly biological theses which composed the sheaf of ideas known as evolutionism to imply any one far-off divine event to which the whole creation moves, nothing to justify speaking of times which are ripe or unripe, nothing to warrant belief in the coming of a crowning race under whose command will be Earth and Earth's. What is there in *The Origin of Species* or *The Descent of Man* to make one think that scientists, who, one supposes, represent this crowning race, are the flower and fruit of the rest of us? Nevertheless the final poem of "In Memoriam" adds to the scientific data a significance felt in its author's imagination. It arises from the poet's ability to visualize concretely the situation as he understands it and to invest it with lyrical overtones.

To do this is neither scientific nor rational. It can best be described as a vision. It was undoubtedly at the time of its publication a deeply moving vision, though our most influential contemporary critic, Mr. T. S. Eliot, finds it "an interesting compromise between the religious attitude and, what is quite a different thing, the belief in human perfectibility." Tennyson, he adds, "has nothing to which to hold fast except his unique and unerring feeling for the sounds of words."[6] Mr. Eliot probably is right, since Tennyson after writing "In Memoriam" said that he thought of adding another poem to it, "bringing out the thoughts of the 'Higher Pantheism' and showing that all the arguments are about as good on one side as the other, and thus throw man back more on the primitive impulses and feelings."[7]

---

[5] See *The Forerunners of Darwin,* ed. by Strauss, Temkin, and Glass (Baltimore: The Johns Hopkins Press, 1959).

[6] "In Memoriam," in *Essays Ancient and Modern* (London: Faber and Faber, 1936), pp. 187 and 189.

[7] Quoted in *The Poetic and Dramatic Works of Alfred Lord Tennyson,*

As a matter of cold fact, the vision which we have referred to was probably stimulated by primitive impulses and feeling to which the poet, like most poets, held fast. The adjective "primitive" may be misleading, but it indicates, however vaguely, that part of our mind which has visions and creates myths. If one of these visions is human perfectibility, that vision becomes religious by its identification with the will of God, though Mr. Eliot may not choose to call it such. For the contradictory, as propounded in certain forms of Christianity —and I realize that Mr. Eliot would deny the propriety of speaking of forms of Christianity, there being only one in his opinion—is also a vision and emerges from primitive impulses and feelings. There is no rational evidence that man is or is not perfectible. Both the assertion and the denial of the possibility are based upon faith and what men have faith in seems to vary from man to man.

Were reason to turn its guns on such a vision, it is clear that it could easily demolish it. For it encompasses a range of speculation far beyond that of experience and, since it is not a set of mathematical theorems, far beyond that of logical implication. Nothing would be easier than to ridicule the idea that all creation is moving toward any particular divine event, for the amount of creation of which we know anything is tiny and the goal is in the so distant future that we can only dream of what it would be like. Some evolutionists might argue that the whale and the other marine mammals are the goal, or that the social insects or the Compositae are the goal. The very notion of "all creation," as if we knew that all creation could be compressed into one formula, could be riddled with objections. But the point of such a vision is to express the nonrational in rational language.

A myth is no more rational than an emblem. It supplements the deficiencies of experience through the imagination. The sight of a tree is nonrational also. To become subject to ra-

ed. by W. J. Rolfe (Boston and New York: Houghton, Mifflin, 1898), p. 832.

tional scrutiny, every item of experience has to be translated into sentences, judgments, assertions, call them what you will. And as long as a man keeps silent when confronted by a new sight, he can neither be refuted nor substantiated. It may not be wise to call such confrontation knowledge, and I would agree, but it is nevertheless the source of knowledge, the stimulus to knowledge, and the fact that it is in itself noncognitive does not render it any the less valuable. For before theory can begin, an hypothesis must be formulated. And an hypothesis rests upon the imagination.

In the long run it will be found that most of our life is conducted by faith, by instinct, by accumulated habit, even by hope. The sphere of reason has a surface to which such directions are at most tangential. The faith that we have in people whom we trust is not necessarily founded on experience; that is why it is so often deceived. But nevertheless it is essential to the organization of even the simplest social group. Our habits or customs, in spite of their compulsive nature, work well only insofar as the past repeats itself; but they help to maintain the past and thus give us cultural stability. Our instincts operate without thought or foresight; we are often at their mercy. But if we had none, living would be consumed with arguing about what we now do automatically. And hope is inherently feeble, since the future to which it is directed may never be realized for us. But a life without hope would be a senseless routine.

One can go through the whole inventory of these non-rational propensities and easily see that the role of reason would become that of a murderer. What reason can one give for living, for loving, for eating, for writing, for speaking to our fellows? The destructive power of detached reason resides in its technique: it can more easily disprove than prove. For the Law of Contradiction is based upon the possibility that every concept will have its correlative and that if P is true, then non-P must be false. It works within strictly limited areas or subject matters and it has long been known that when it tackles the universal, it faces defeat. Logically, as we have said above, when a term is so inflated that its denotation becomes really universal, it loses all distinctive meaning. That is a tautology. But if we hanker after universals, we must admit that we can reach them only through metaphor or myth.

None of this is said in deprecation of reasoning. It is the one corrective which we have of aspirations which will be inevitably frustrated. But sometimes, since reason works with premises drawn from experience, its conclusions will be as limited as the experience on which it is based. There is a famous case in the history of science which illustrates how a sound practice arose from a false theory. Before the discovery of the bacillus of malaria, it was believed that the disease was carried on the miasmas arising from the swamps as the day grew cooler. Consequently it was prescribed that people ought to avoid breathing in the night air and they were ordered to sleep with their windows closed. Doing so, they excluded not only the night air from their bedrooms but also the anopheles mosquito. Rationally this was a good enough technique, for air was one of the few things, not food or drink, which we drew into our bodies from without. The normal margin of error would account for those cases in which the preventive measures failed. If we had no way of extending our experience through the imagination, we should still be living in what Mr. Lewis Mumford called the eotechnic period. How absurd to think that by striking flint against a bit of metal anything so unlike flint or metal as fire would ensue! Why should anyone put little hard pellets into the ground and expect them to turn into plants? And why should the excrement of animals, clearly that which the beast could not digest, aid in the growth of vegetables? The commonest of our practices seem like folly once we divest ourselves of the accumulated knowledge of the past. But no matter how far advanced we are on the path to omniscience, our range of knowledge is still very limited. When men began to develop aeronautics, they assumed that because air was a fluid, the theorems of aerodynamics would be identical with those of hydrodynamics. They were wrong.

But after all they had to be proved wrong by the failure of their applied science, not by the natural assumptions which they had made. It was the desire to fly, not the reasonableness of flight, which led to success. This, as I say, is an old story, but like many old stories its moral is often forgotten. It is doubtful whether a single discovery or invention could not be shown to be rationally impossible before it is made. For historically the possible is what has already been accomplished and new possibilities may often be actualized through accident, dogged persistence, stubborn hope and faith.

Myth is a step beyond metaphor in making our ideas concrete. The event which is transformed into a myth retains its temporal dimension since a myth is always a narrative. Expressed overtly in human terms, it gains emotive power and clothes the bare body of fact with the robes of art and religion. Though it cannot be verified when recognized as a myth, it will always be called upon to round out a body of ideas, for any system of thought will sooner or later reach the point where "ultimate" questions are raised.

5

Concentrated Emblems

THE EMOTIONAL AURA WHICH SURROUNDS certain common terms, such as The Flag, Mother, Liberty, Truth, Beauty, which we have called significance, may surround even more abstract terms, such as Nature, Law, Order, and Form. This is what Professor A. O. Lovejoy has called *metaphysical pathos*.[1] Usually we think of agreeable and disagreeable feelings as attached to persons, events, and things, rather than to ideas and the words which name them. But no matter how general and abstract a word may be, it can assume an almost magical property of inducing people who are attracted to it to use it as a term of praise.

One of the most famous of such terms is "nature" and its derivatives. That which is natural in any one of its many meanings is supposed to be inherently better than the unnatural, as the lawful is better than the unlawful, the orderly better than the disorderly. To declare something unnatural is supposed by lovers of nature to denounce and condemn it without further argument. Unnatural mothers, unnatural vice, and even unnatural murder, as in *Hamlet,* are held to be worse than natural mothers, vice, and murder. Similarly in aesthetic criticism one finds the word "form" used as if all one had to do to condemn a work of art was to point out that it was "formless," in spite of the fact that everything has some form whether we have a name for it or not.

If one were to argue with people who are attracted by

[1] See his *The Great Chain of Being* (Harper Torchbooks, 1960), p. 11.

nature, one could easily show that one of the differentiae of man is to be unnatural, in the sense that he can change the natural order and usually does so. In such an argument one would mean by the natural order the order in which the animals are believed to live, an order of life guided by instinct and routine. The intervention of human ingenuity in so changing things that men are happier in them has been one of those things which have made civilization, and, even if one finds fault with civilization, if one looks back with longing to an epoch in which men lived a simple and uncivilized life, one would be hard put to it to discover a community in which there are no artifacts, no fire, no tribal customs, no magic. The more reasonable conclusion would be that it is man's nature to do things which the animals do not do and then to appraise such things on their own merits. But one of the meanings of "the natural" is "the regular," the usual and the customary, and to say that something is unnatural denotes in that case that it is rare or contrary to custom. The paradox here—for in all instances of metaphysical pathos there is a paradoxical element—is that rarity is also used as a standard of excellence. Things, it appears, can be excellent only if they are outstandingly above other things of the class to which they normally belong. And the man who praises someone for his naturalness is also just as likely to point out that he excels in that trait.

The ambiguity of the word "nature" is typical of all words which have powerful emotional auras. The word is first used to name something or other and also to praise it. Then it would look as if its denotation was overlooked and it is applied to almost everything which one admires. Its opposites are used for opposite effects. Now that "democracy" has taken on a eulogistic flavor, both the Russians and the Americans use it to name their political and social institutions. The word itself, regardless of what it names, becomes an emblem of something either liked or hated, and just as superstitious Huguenots in the Wars of Religion mutilated the statues of the saints in the Catholic churches, so sacred words themselves will be treated with a kind of respect usually given only to human beings. This transfer of significance from things to their names is not so unusual as to excite wonder. It is analogous to the veneration paid to relics, not merely relics of the saints and martyrs, but to those of parents and friends, locks of hair, for instance, at one time being hoarded as if they were surrogates for the persons on whose head they grew. Booksellers can ask higher prices for association copies of books than for the same books which are not association copies. Autograph letters, signatures, furniture, and jewelry, which are found in private and indeed public collections, seem to have a value which is not that of the material objects themselves but of the person who wrote them or to whom they belonged. Just as some words are decent and indecent, regardless of their meanings—for one can always use a Greek or Latin derivative for an indecent Anglo-Saxon word meaning the same thing—so some are sacred and some profane regardless of their meaning. They contain rolled up in them a wealth of vague but powerful emotions—for which mixed metaphor I apologize—very much as the old Chinese ivory balls used to contain smaller balls which seemed to continue *ad infinitum*.

It will be recalled that in some societies, and those not the most primitive, the exact form of words is held to have a power which even the slightest change would weaken. This obtains of course in magical formulas, in charms, and in religious ritual. It is not the meaning of the phrases which is involved here but the actual words. It will also be recalled that the names of persons and gods take on a magical power and sometimes the name is so sacred that it must not be pronounced at all. In Captain Cook's voyages among the Polynesians, he discovered that the exchange of names was a special mark of consideration, and in some countries it has become almost habitual to perpetuate the father's name by giving it to one of his sons or the mother's family name by using that instead of a "given" name. This is done not because there is any peculiar beauty to the name; in fact, at times the combination of given and family names becomes absurd. But the passing along from one generation to the next of something which seems to arrest the passage of time, something which looks like a tradition, appears to solace some people for the dangers of mutability. So in political affairs a word or phrase may acquire such significance that it is risky to attempt to define its meaning. How many Americans today would publicly question the meaning of "democracy," "freedom," "self-government," or even "The People"?

Sometimes the significance of words and phrases makes a complete reversal. The eternal, the everlasting, the immutable, for instance, have in the minds of some men been replaced by the dynamic, the creative, the vital, just as the unified, the coherent, the simple, have been replaced by the richness of complexity, the organic, the growing. And when people want to eat their cake and have it too, we come upon unity in variety, coherent heterogeneity, and dynamic tension. Where such a philosopher as St. Thomas Aquinas sees nobility in the logical form of the universe, another, such as Schelling, sees it in the interplay of freedom and determinism, positive and negative, and so on. Some of the German romantic philosophers felt that any restraints on the creative will would be evil and they laid down as their program striving for the sake of striving. To other philosophers, for instance Plato and Aristotle, the will was under the command of the reason and, in Plato's case, the possibility of what ends could be sought was strictly limited by the World of Ideals. If reason alone were involved and if the premises of a rational system were self-evident, these conflicts ought not to obtain.

Now an historian can point out that sometimes old words lose their magic and, as we have suggested, their contraries take their place. Our emphasis today upon the organic, the vital, the creative, is something new. Though one can find instances of ancient philosophers who approached this usage, I know of none who reached it. The Stoics, for instance, spoke of the Cosmos as a Great Animal permeated by something which they called Spirit (*Pneuma*) which like the Phoenix was born out of its ashes and lived only to be consumed in a universal conflagration. But the procedure was regular and contained no novelty as one Great Year was succeeded by another. To contemplate the eternal recurrence in one's imagination was presumably a comfort to the Stoic Sage, but to a man like Shelley, who has given us one of the clearest poetic descriptions of this event, it was more depressing than elating.

> Oh cease! must hate and death return?
> Cease! must men kill and die?
> Cease! drain not to its dregs the urn
> Of bitter prophecy.
> The world is weary of the past,
> Oh, might it die or rest at last!

But to be weary of the past, though no doubt a common enough feeling in at least the young, was not a sentiment which the classic philosophers were likely to express. The belief that the future was an endless repetition of the past was what gave order and dependableness to history, and impatience with tradition was characteristic of thoughtless young men.

Shelley, however, stood at the point where new ideas were beginning to make themselves felt. "Hellas," the poem from which the verses quoted come, was written in Pisa in 1821. It was the time of rebellion in the states of Italy, as well as of the Spanish Revolution. One has only to read Shelley's preface to the poem to see what inspired it. It surely requires no proof to say that revolutions are made to change the existing order and they rest upon the hope that the new order will be better than the old. By 1821 both the American and the French Revolutions had occurred and had been successful, though the latter had already met with disaster, first at the hands of Napoleon and then at those of the Bourbons. There is a curious indication of feelings of men at that time in the words of a relatively obscure French philosopher, the Abbé Bautain. He said that his generation could not believe that the human will was to be completely at the mercy of external influences, for they had seen one great will, that of the Emperor, at work. Napoleon had become for the youth of the early nineteenth century in France a symbol of a creative—and destructive—will. If Hegel could describe him as the world spirit on horseback, it was because he seemed perfectly to incarnate a kind of power unlimited by anything beyond itself. Napoleon to the men who admired him was an anticipation of Nietzsche's Superman and it was one of the peculiarities of the Superman to listen to no will but his own. He did not seek values, he created them.

The revolutions in politics during the first half of the nineteenth century were paralleled by revolutions in science. Dalton's atomic theory was formed in the first years of the century. Faraday was working on his electrical experiments in the twenties and published his results in the forties. Evolutionism was gradually captivating the minds of biologists and also, as we have suggested, of philosophers. Historical knowledge was pushed farther back by the excavations in Pompeii after 1814 and the deciphering of the Rosetta stone in 1821. It could hardly be imagined after these and similar novelties that history was nothing but the repetition of the same events. The old tradition of discounting time was broken and, one suspects, broken for good and all. None of this proved that as time went on things moved from good to better to best, but at least it showed that they moved. The acceptance of time as a reality which could not be explained away was the achievement of twentieth-century philosophy, but it had its start in the actual innovations of the nineteenth. The additional element of progress, in the sense of history's always moving toward the better, was probably the fruit of the biological theory of evolution, for if man were the apex of biological progress, no man would deny that the direction was toward the good. Pride of race was unquestioned, as it usually is. And few men were capable of looking at themselves and saying that if this was what the struggle was for, it was hardly worth the effort.

It had long been a custom to identify the real and the good. When real things were contrasted with imaginary things, with dreams, with illusions, it was clear that people would normally prefer the real. But when one turned the adjective "real" into a noun "reality," one had also to transfer the significance of the adjective to the noun. When only the immutable and the timeless were real, only they were good, and men were warned not to linger in the temporal and mutable world, but to seek salvation in the world of the eternal and unchanging. Similarly when men began to accept time, they inclined toward endowing it with all the virtue which the timeless once had had, and in the works of some philosophers, such as William James, God Himself was in process of becoming. Since Fichte had said that the real is not what is but what ought to be, philosophers could push the divine existence into an infinitely distant future, which would be like a mathematical limit toward which things are moving but which they would never reach. It may have been some such impulse that directed men toward surrounding the changing, the dynamic, and the evolving with that atmosphere of beauty which made it—or them— the standard of goodness. Be that as it may, we now are in a situation where these are adjectives of praise and to say that something is static is automatically to set it well down in the scales of values. The shift has come about not from reasoning, unless one assumes *a priori* that whatever is, is right, and hence concludes that if the world is temporal, then the temporal is good. But no one ever reasoned in so clear-cut a fashion to a universal standard of goodness, not even Alexander Pope who first put the axiom into books of familiar quotations.

Whatever is, need not be either right or wrong. It may simply be. To have analyzed the traits of Being, in the sense of the most universal existents, is to have achieved an intellectual goal well worth achieving, but it is not self-evident that one has also constructed a theory of value. A theory of value must have other than simply existential premises. Change may be for better or worse, creation may be of evil as well as of good, life may be hideous as well as beautiful, just as evil may be everlasting, unified, and universal. One can presumably explain why human beings value the things which they do value. One can explain why some people value one kind of thing and others another. One might even be able to convince a man that his scheme of valuation is wrong. But I fail to see how, without introducing a premise which would induce one into begging the question, one could ever deduce value from fact, goodness from existence.

The Ancients, for instance, were in general convinced that *autarky* of the individual was the highest good. The man who had reached a point of complete self-dependence, independence of all external goods, was sovereign and free. The ethical schools, Epicureans, Stoics, Skeptics, and Platonists, all agreed on this point and disagreed only on how to acquire this freedom from wants. *Autarky*, like nature, became a magic word. Its function in thinking was not unlike that of the word "freedom" today. Men who speak of freedom seldom tell us what we are to be free from or for. If the antithesis of freedom is restraint, then our bodies, other people, food and drink, space and time are all on the side of the line which divides freedom from nonfreedom. For each of them restrains us in limiting our possibilities. Indeed one could interpret history as the uninterrupted attempt on the part of man to free himself from the inevitable restraints which nature has put upon him. But again, to pronounce the word "freedom" is to say something sacred. In the same way, I can think of no Greek philosopher, except possibly some of the Sophists, who did not take it for granted that *autarky* was the highest good. To be free of all needs, to lack nothing, was a good which they thought required no defense.

We do not know enough about the causes of happiness and unhappiness to decide whether the sacred words indicate what men feel the want of or whether they acquire their sanctity through some other cause. But whatever may be said of the Greeks who did not write books, we can say that those who did would hardly have been so determined in their search for *autarky* as they were, unless it was something which they missed in their own lives. Their criticism of their fellows is usually based on the common desire for things which will prove to be only a restraint on their individual sovereignty. Such things were love of wealth, overweening ambition, the excessive pursuit of pleasure, the desire for knowing more than they should, all of which would lead to enslavement.

I do not say that these were the only targets of Greek moral criticism or that nothing other than the abandonment of *autarky* was criticized. But as far as the main ethical philosophies were concerned, they looked to the attainment of independence as the one goal worth striving for. In Epicureanism it came through peace of mind accompanying freedom from pain; in Stoicism through apathy or freedom from emotional involvement in worldly affairs; in Skepticism through the admission of ignorance; and in Platonism through the intellectual contemplation of the eternal ideas. It is difficult to believe that such philosophies were not the result of a profound dissatisfaction with things as they were. That Hellenistic philosophies turned to mysticism and even to superstition is not surprising. Their practitioners found little this side of eternity to help them out of the morass of time and change. Otherwise it seems strange that they should have urged their followers to cut off all social ties, including in the case of the early Cynics, marriage itself.

The emotional effect of a word or sentence cannot come from its sound alone. Nor can an abstraction in isolation, such as the binomial theorem or the equation for a parabola, have any emotional aura. It is only the concrete which can stimulate emotions, so that when one find a highly abstract term invested with strong emotional power, it must be that the men who feel it think of the term in some concrete exemplification. It is at this point that myth makes its contribution. Without attempting any general explanation of the rise of metaphysical pathos which will be correct step by step, since all the aspects of an idea, denotational as well as connotational, arise together, we can say with some degree of accuracy that the abstractions which we have been considering are precipitated into concretions as follows:

First—and again let me say that I am not speaking of chronological priority—one has the contribution of tradition. One is educated into thinking highly of unity or variety, stability or change, the natural or the vital or the organic or the mechanical. One reads books in which whatever is named by such terms is said to be better than other things. One hears them used as terms of praise, as if there were no question about their eulogistic connotation.

None of this would stand up under logical criticism, but nevertheless the usage gives one a comfortable feeling of belonging to a great tradition, of carrying forward the banners of one's ancestral tribe, of fighting for what the race has always stood for, of participating in a collective soul, of simple and naïve agreement with one's fellows. The human animal has never been averse to such social involvement. There is not only utilitarian value in it but also terminal value. It is not a trivial matter that the hermit is an exception to the general rule. The individual gets definite satisfaction in being identified with the group and the group gets sustenance from the individual's willingness to be identified with it. No group wants to commit suicide.

Second, the abstraction becomes consolidated into an emblem. A hieroglyph or icon of the abstraction is formed. There are of course certain emblems, such as those of sixteenth-century Italian jurist, Andrea Alciati, which are deliberately invented. Heraldry, both genuine and not, gives us good example of conventional emblems. There may be some relation to totemism in the more ancient emblems of certain tribes, such as the eagle and the snake of Mexico, but sometimes a pun upon the name of the person bearing the arms is used. If Sir Stephen Cheyndut bears an oak tree, and Candavène bears oats, one does not have to go far to find the source of the emblem. Even the *fleur-de-lis* has been seen as a pun on the name of Louis (Loys). But sometimes it is possible that certain things have an inherent psychic concomitant, though this is dubious, for it has been held that a given color is associated with a special type of event because it provokes the mood supposed to be peculiar to that event, black standing for mourning, blue for hope, yellow for jealousy. It would really make little difference whether the mood were generally evoked by the color or not, for custom would suffice. If the Koreans use white for mourning and the tribes of Dahomey red, we cannot say that the colors and the emotions which we correlate with them are bound together by psychological laws, unless we are also willing to say that those people who do not feel as we do about the colors in question are not human.

The consolidation of an abstraction into an emblem becomes more complicated when the emblem in question is something intimately bound up with an historical event of great importance. Such traditional signs as the Cross or the Star of David have become more than indicators of religious affiliation. The Cross contains within it the whole concept of vicarious atonement by the incarnated God, a mystery which can be talked about but which cannot adequately be expressed in words. It is not enough to say that it was the instrument on which Jesus was tortured to death, for to a Christian this would leave out its religious significance. It has become a sacred object, not simply an instrument of torture, like the gallows or thumbscrew. Meditation upon it leads to an exfoliation of ideas which are not resident in it as a material object; they are found only when it is thought of as a material object enveloped in emotion. One man will write,

> Christian, up and smite them,
> Counting gain but loss;
> Smite them by the merit
> Of the holy Cross.

Another will write,

> But on his breast a bloody cross he bore,
> The dear remembrance of his dying Lord.

Elizabeth Barrett Browning wrote,

> O Christians, at your cross of hope, a hopeless hand
> was clinging!

And Francis Thompson,

> He the Anteros and Eros,
> I the body, he the Cross . . .

And Alexander Pope,

> On her white breast a sparkling cross she wore
> Which Jews might kiss, and infidels adore.

Any dictionary of quotations will provide dozens of other examples of how a given emblem may contain within itself a multitude of diverse meanings: hope, desire for revenge, mystic union, and even satire.

A third source of consolidated emblems is the representation visually of a metaphor. We are all familiar with the All-seeing Eye of God which appears on documents as a human eye with rays shooting out from it. As part of the great seal of the United States it appears in fact on dollar bills. I confess not to knowing the historical origin of this emblem, but one imagines that first God was thought of as omniscient and therefore as observing all cosmic affairs as if He had an eye; He was then identified with the Eye, and then the Eye alone sufficed to wrap up the entire idea with all its ramifications. On a less lofty plane we have the anchor as a symbol of hope, or the eagle as a symbol of power. If anyone had sat down first to reflect on the possible implications of some such symbols, he might have seen their double meanings, the anchor holding the ship in place, the eagle being a bird of prey as well as the high flying creature which alone, according to legend, looks the sun in the face. But needless to say, no one ever did sit down to fabricate such emblems. And no one knows really when and where they began their careers. But on the other hand, every time a man devises his bookplate or a group of men design a shield or crest for a fraternity, or even for a grocery store, some thought is first given to what is to be expressed. The results may be ludicrous, as when a Boston grocer used as his motto, *Luxuria cum economia*. But the need for a concrete image of a program or any other idea is satisfied in a visual image, however absurd the words which may accompany it.

All emblems, whatever their genesis, are subject to what might be called the Law of the Petrification of Forms. Just as architectural details which start by being functional remain as decoration, witness the structure of the stone temples of Greece which are built as if they were of wood, the various residues of medieval fortified castles which can still be seen on college buildings, or the broken pediments which are now found even on billboards, highboys, and mirrors, so any emblem which may have begun as a deliberate concrete representation of an abstraction will remain as part and parcel of the common idiom. When Michelangelo represents God, he pictures Him as an old bearded and powerful man. One never, to the best of my knowledge, sees the Creator as a powerful youth or a Mother. It is true that the Third Commandment may have proved an inhibiting influence upon the imagination of artists. But in spite of this prohibition, artists continued to represent God, and He was always pictured as an old man, presumably a father, just as He is addressed in the Lord's Prayer. Protests such as that of Xenophanes in the sixth century B.C. against even thinking of God as if He were a human being, or that of Philo Judaeus in the last pre-Christian century, or all the works of the Patristic theologians, were futile as far as painting was concerned.

But this was to be expected. We know enough about the history of our vocabulary to remember how words themselves become petrified, frozen as of a certain date, even though their meaning changes. The life of a symbol is in the minds of the people who use it, for they alone can vitalize it. Consequently, the continued appearance of a word over a long period of years does not permit us to infer that it retains its original meaning. We still use such words as "philosophy," "art," "religion," regardless of how their meaning has shifted from what it was primarily.[2] A glance at the *New English Dictionary* will convince anyone who needs to be convinced that no matter how much a meaning may change, an old word will usually be retained to express it. To argue from the etymology of a word like "philosophy" that its proper meaning is "the love of wisdom," is to overlook the demonstrable fact that no word has a proper meaning contained within it, unless it is a neologism which has had so short a life that it has not had time to become ambiguous. But while the word, as so many letters or such and such a sound, remains fixed, its significance as well as its denotation may change. I have already mentioned words which once were decent and later became indecent, and there are a few, like "subjective" and "objective," which have exchanged meanings. For those who think I am exaggerating the fluidity of meaning and significance, I should recommend a reading of Matthew Arnold's lectures on translating Homer and his subsequent debate with Newman on the same subject.

So far I have been talking about emblems which may have been established by convention. But it would be folly to overlook the contributions of the Unconscious. For after all if the Occident as a whole accepts the idea of God as a father, it must be because there is a need for a supernatural father felt by most Occidentals. And if a great number of them also speak of Christ as the Redeemer, it must be because they have a sense of sin and feel the need of redemption. I do not say that every individual in the West feels these two needs, but nevertheless they lie deep within even those of us who are not professing Jews or Christians and they emerge into consciousness when we feel a sense of loneliness, of estrangement from an un-

[2] Cf. R. B. Onians; *The Origins of European Thought about the Body, the Mind, the Soul, the World, Time, and Fate* (Cambridge, at the University Press, 1951).

named being whom we dare not name, or of guilt when we are troubled by something which we have or have not done. It is possible that all this can be explained by psychiatry, by the residues of childhood instruction, by a repressed desire for self-expression, by the Oedipus complex, by our resentments toward social pressures. But whatever the explanation, the feelings are there and express themselves in traditional speech and myth.

Alongside of these symbols are some of a more personal type which float into the consciousness of individuals, they know not how or why, but which are more moving than others which might be more approved of by society. Even in so basic a matter as sexual attraction, men vary in what stimulates them and there is no sense in universalizing the beauty of women, as if any woman would do for any man to fall in love with. If one's experience in barracks and smoking rooms does not suffice to prove this, one has only to make a collection of paintings of female nudes beginning with the Italian Renaissance and going down to Picasso to see how styles in women change. Yet if there were one thing which might be expected to be uniform, it would be sexual attraction. On a less obvious plane, one can take an artist like Matisse or Picasso or Miró and see the repeated use of certain forms and movements in their paintings and sculptures which apparently have become compulsive and whose emotional power, even if it comes down to mere pleasantness, must be of some felt value. This repetition of forms is to be found in the doodling which people who are far from being artists engage in while thinking of something else; the doodles of one man are characteristic of him and not of all men.

Much art is a concealment of motivation rather than a revelation of it, in spite of talk about art as communication. If something is persistently concealed or expressed—and nothing can be permanently concealed from the psychiatrist—it is probably because of the emotional satisfaction of doing one or the other. Since the concealing of an interest, either by repression or by disguising it through substitutions, is in all likelihood due to anticipated social censure, one must always take into account, when considering any kind of symbolism—myths, emblems, metaphors, or what you will—the influence of society on the individual's way of thinking. In this context one may have consolidated abstractions running all the way from the socially approved to the socially reproved. And concomitantly with these one will have emblems which on one extreme will be easily read by anyone and on the other those which are hermetically sealed within the person of him who uses them.

In the earlier days of Freud's popularity a whole lexicon of symbols was drawn up and used by writers. Freud himself pointed out that the reference of a symbol could be determined only by an examination of the individual using it. Ladders, chimneys, plumes, caves, forests, and all the rest did of course have some sexual reference and a reference which the person dreaming of them and building fantasies round them might not be aware of. But then all symbolism was held to have sexual reference and consequently simply to say that something was a phallic symbol or a symbol of the mother's womb, was too general to explain why one man was haunted by mountain peaks and another by furled umbrellas. Popular writers on psychoanalysis overlooked Freud's own strictures on such interpretations and oddly enough we had the paradoxical situation of deeply personal emblems getting their meaning fixed by the literary expositions of Freud. Similarly the Jungian archetypes became general human emblems which in their case were lodged not in the individual's unconscious in isolation from that of other people, but in what was called the collective unconscious. But insofar as general agreement on the inherent significance of the symbols was induced through literature, the poet or dramatist or painter or architect discovered that far from concealing those ideas of which he was frightened or ashamed—which amounts to about the same thing—he was revealing them not to the specialist, for no specialists existed, but to everyone. The Unconscious is not any more foolish than the Conscious and recourse to archetypes as a disguise became futile.

Similar to the emblems of psychoanalysis are those which have been interpreted by Marxians and Pseudo-Marxians. Here it is not erotic emblems which are in question but economic. When a critic of painting points out that painters of the early cubist period utilized the odds and ends lying about in their studios as subject matter, instead of painting symbols of the class struggle, he was likely to interpret this practice as an evasion of responsibility. The guitars, fans, old newspapers, bottles, and bits of music which were put together to form a flat pattern were not deliberately selected, it was said, because the artist wished to show his irresponsibility, but because the artist felt no responsibility to his fellow workers. Hence he painted these trivialities. It could also have been said, though I recall no one's saying it, that by breaking them up into fragments and then using the fragments as elements in his design, he was showing his contempt for *la vie de Bohème* and indirectly his allegiance to the program of the proletarian revolution.

This technique of interpretation may serve a variety of purposes. One can say that when a painter paints game, fish, bottles of wine, and the other furniture of still-lifes, his thoughts rise no higher than his stomach. If, on the contrary, he paints a Crucifixion, an Annunciation, a Resurrection, he can be said to have evaded his terrestrial obligations and taken refuge in other-worldliness. If he paints portraits of the men and women who can afford to pay for them, he can then be accused of identifying himself with the capitalistic class. If, like some of the academic painters of the nineteenth century, he paints "ideal heads," then it is because he cannot face reality. I am not denying the existence of unconscious causes of our choice of subject matter, and I realize that they operate well beyond the field of the fine arts, but I am insisting that only a psychiatrist can determine what these causes are in any particular case.

One cannot and should not prevent people from interpreting

works of art as they wish. For no work of art emits its meaning like the cry of a bird, but requires interpretation. What has been called the aesthetic experience is a function of both the work of art and the onlooker, the reader, the listener. It is not, in spite of the unfortunate word "aesthetic," a purely sensory experience and, even if it were, each interpreter would use his own code to make its meaning clear to himself. When one reads into a picture or poem or building one's own meaning, one is of course helpless to do otherwise, but that is no reason for reading into the artist's mind the effect of his work upon oneself. His intentions may be said at most to be the making of that particular work of art, and what other intentions are imputed to him are the result of conjecture. The artist may have learned ways of affecting others which are successful in achieving the result which he has planned, the aim of amusing, of depressing, of teaching, of arguing, of satirizing, of eulogizing, to take only a few of the most frequent aims of artistry. But because a spectator of a picture sees it as amusing is no proof that the artist intended it to be amusing. The nudes of William Blake, for instance, have muscles but no bones; are we to suppose that they were purposely drawn that way? The comic scenes in *Macbeth* do not strike some of us as really very funny; but everyone is agreed that they were intended to be funny. For that matter Shylock may very well have been intended by Shakespeare to be a comic character; but who today thinks of him as comic? Sometimes, it must be granted, the artist's intentions and the spectator's interpretation agree and sometimes they do not agree. It is always pleasant to have fathomed another man's purposes, but when the other man is dead or of an exotic culture, one may just as well be resigned to not fathoming them.

As a final example of emblems intended or unintended, we might take the case of some whose meanings are not as yet fixed. Is abstract and nonobjective painting a rejection of life? Is it the expression of tensions which are supposed to exist in modern society as they do in modern man? Is it a reflection of physics which some have said to be the physics of function rather than of substance? Is it an attempt on the part of artists to bring painting closer to music? Here one cannot go to the artist and ask him, for what painters write is usually unintelligible for the simple reason that painters are not writers. Here then is an art to which meaning must be given, for to date there is no meaning generally agreed upon in the movement of lines and masses and the interaction of colors. People who are impatient with such painting say that it is meaningless, when they do not say that it is deliberate mystification. Their annoyance at not finding what they expect to find leads them to overlook what may be there.

No one, to the best of my knowledge, ever objected to looking at a fall of snow, at autumn leaves, at the swirling of water, at contour plowing from the air, at the texture of rocks, at wavering reflections in pools, at the striations of shells, at the grain of wood, at clouds moving across the sky, or at photographs of microscopic organisms. These phenomena may mean something to the physicist, the biologist, the agriculturist, but people need not be scientists or technicians to take pleasure in just looking at them. Why then, when patterns which are similar to these are transferred to canvas, should they become annoying, not to say infuriating? The answer probably is, Because tradition is against it. When we hear a word, we expect it to be the vehicle of intelligible meaning; we seldom hear it simply as a sound. It is only by great effort that we can dissociate its meaning from its sound and most of us do not bother to take the trouble. Yet one suspects that if one translated most poetry into prose and jotted down only what it says, it would seem either trivial or false.

But one cannot always translate poetry into prose. Here is the opening of one of Shakespeare's best-known sonnets:

> When to the sessions of sweet silent thought
> I summon up remembrance of things past . . .

Does this mean merely, "When I try to recall the past"? Is the

juridical metaphor of no importance? If not, should we translate, "When I bring into court my recollections"? But what of
the "court of thought"? Is it again of no importance that the
writer is both the accused and the judge? If not, should we
translate, "When I make an examination of conscience"? Before long one throws up the sponge and leaves the lines as they
were written, for even the alliteration and the tempo of the
rhythm begin to count. But this will be true of any work of art.
To translate a poem into prose is no more or less possible than
to translate a picture or a building or a piece of music into
prose. There is no problem of translating some verse into prose
for it is simply prose in doggerel form.

> Lives of great men all remind us
> We can make our lives sublime . . .

There is clearly nothing here that is not prose except the meter.
But in the opening of Shakespeare's sonnet, whether one
admire it or not, there has been compacted a meaning which
to make explicit would require paragraphs. And those paragraphs would strike a reader with all the force and majesty of
a leaking spigot.

The basic difficulty is that such works of art are not essentially
discursive, but contain meanings implicit within them which
we somehow or other find emerging as we look, listen, or read.
The rapidity of this is analogous to the sudden discovery by a
scientist of a satisfactory hypothesis. He has looked at a collection of facts which he believes to contain a hidden unity. His
mind is troubled by the conflict between his faith that the
unity can be found and yet does not appear. Then—and this
is an old story—there suddenly flashes into his mind a law, a
generalization, an hypothesis which works and binds together
all the apparent diversity. A similar thing takes place when one
is studying something hard. One puzzles over the texts and
again the solution flashes into one's mind and everything is
seen in its proper relation to everything else. The distinctive
difference between this sort of experience and the aesthetic ex-

perience is the directions of the processes. Looking at a painting
or reading a poem is a single and almost unitary experience
which develops into multiplicity; finding a scientific hypothesis
or grasping a law which underlies a multiplicity of data begins
with variety and ends with unity. Both of these sentences are
only partly true, since no picture was ever so simple that it did
not contain some variety and no set of scientific data is so
heterogeneous that its members are not somewhat alike, for
otherwise they would not be considered together. Moreover, in
the case of works of art it takes some time before the eye can
be trained to see everything which is in them. Synoptic vision
is not given at birth. But, as in all other situations in which
training is needed, the actual steps of the learned process drop
out of consciousness and we interpret at once what is before
us. People have to learn bit by bit how to talk their own
language and understand a foreign language, but once these
things are learned, they seem to take no time. It is very likely
that a taxonomist behaves similarly when he spots a strange
animal or plant. He sees in it the species or genus to which it is
customarily allocated and only later begins to reflect on what
he has seen. Where the early biological systematizers worked
from obvious morphological similarities, their modern suc-
cessors are more interested in phylogeny. The individual specimen becomes a symbol of the whole class to which it belongs,
just as the picture, poem, or piece of music stands for a cultural
period, a style, an artistic "movement."

Suppose now someone were to ask, "What is the baroque?"
or, "What is an elephant?" The best reply would be either the
production of an example of each or, in view of the difficulty
of producing them, a photograph of some baroque church or
an elephant. Verbal descriptions are plentiful, but they are
much more opaque than the actual objects themselves. The
clarity of the visual is what is wanted, not the precision of the
verbal. Seeing an elephant or a baroque church is, when one
stops to think about it, as superficial a way of knowing anything
about them as one could discover. For what interests a biologist

in elephants is not merely what they look like but what is inside their skin, and what interests an historian of art in the baroque is not merely the glitter and the gold but, to take a single detail, the movement of light and dark. A person innocent of art history may see the movement of light and dark planes on the façade of a baroque palace or church without noticing it as anything of special interest. So a person without biological training may see both a tapir and an elephant in a zoo, actually notice a certain resemblance between them, and think no more of it.

It is obvious that the ability to see resemblances comes first from an interest in them and that interest is awakened by studies which emphasize their importance. My point is that the similarities which are the first steps toward understanding are looked for and one looks for them in order to group things together; one wants the groupings because of previously acquired interests and the groupings which one makes are made to satisfy such interests. If this examination of motives is pushed far enough, one comes out with the conclusion that the fundamental interest, that which orients all inquiry, is the satisfaction of the demands of reason.

6

The Demands of Reason

THERE ARE THREE DEMANDS OF REASON: FIRST, to identify everything in what Poincaré called a cascade of equations; second, to show that everything is linked together in a causal chain; third, to establish an invariant network of relations between things.

Each of these demands is met by a radical simplification of experience. To identify obviously different things is to abstract from them that which differentiates them and the first step toward such simplification is the application of common nouns, or, what amounts to the same thing, classification. The establishment of causal chains is equally a simplification, for when one seeks the cause of a given effect or the effect of a given cause, one not only has to classify but to establish artificial conditions under which the efficacy of the cause can be settled. The third demand is met by singling out specific classes of experience and noting the pattern which they exhibit. This was Newton's great achievement in the *Principia*. He thought of the sun and the planets as exemplifications of mass and of their interrelations as that only of distance. With these two variables he was able to work out a formula which would apply to the phenomena in question with almost perfect accuracy. But the sun and the planets are clearly more than masses and there happen to be astronomers who are interested in some of the remaining characters, for example, their chemical composition, the atmosphere which surrounds them, and in at least two cases, Mars and Venus, their capability of sustaining life.

These three demands all make a further demand, that whatever is said about the subject matter of reason be logically consistent. Logical consistency is obedience to the Law of Contradiction and this cannot be observed unless, first, the sentences which are being tested refer to timeless things, and, second, the words used in them be univalent. As we have already insisted, things and events cannot be consistent or inconsistent; those adjectives apply to propositions, assertions, and sentences. If all change were arrested and a description set up of a group of phenomena, it is possible that such a description might be internally consistent. But if there is one characteristic of the world as we know it which cannot be eliminated, it is change. The basic alteration of experience made by the reason is the rejection of change, for even when curves of change and patterns of change are drawn up, they have to be in such general terms that they become static portraits. There is nothing wrong with this unless someone asserts that mutability is in the formula as well as in the events.

The rational portrait of things is an escape from the changing variety of direct experience. Its simplification is a step toward intelligibility. Whether one call the sciences ideal constructions or works of art makes little difference if one is not too sensitive to the associations of the words. Whatever they are called, they are not and cannot be a photograph of what is going on. They cannot even be true to experience unless by "true" one mean consistent. They are true to purified and simplified experience, experience purified of its variations and simplified by the eradication of individuality. The rules of scientific exploration are established to achieve the satisfaction of one of our strongest desires, the desire for understanding. But understanding is a human desire and is satisfied in the lives of human beings, not in some superhuman system of eternal essences. Its criteria, insofar as there is general agreement about them, are of the same type as the criteria of satisfactory metaphors and myths. In all three analogies are sought and found; in all three emotions are aroused and appeased. The most striking difference is that as one moves in the direction of the sciences the human equation is more and more suppressed.

There was a certain truth in Comte's description of how thought matures, passing from the theological, through the metaphysical, to the positivistic phase. The theological account of changes rests on the operations of an anthropomorphic will. Omit the anthropomorphic traits and speak about forces, and you have a metaphysical science. Omit the forces and observe their operations alone, and you come out with positivistic descriptions. This does not make a positivistic description any truer in the sense of corresponding to fact than a theological description. To say that God created the world *ex nihilo* or that the world has always existed is not to answer a single question. There is nothing absurd in saying that the world had no beginning in time nor is there anything absurd in saying that God created it. The absurdity in either sentence is in the obscurity of the terms. A single and unique event is inexplicable, can neither be caused nor be everlasting nor anything else. It can be talked about only insofar as it differs from other events. Hence to the extent that one man's experience is different from that of all other men, to that extent it is inexplicable and ineffable.

The heterogeneity and mutability of experience have always proved disagreeable to people. By stuffing the multiplicity of things into the sphere of reason, one constructs a world in which one can live in peace. It acquires clarity, simplicity, order, unity, and eternality. But all that is purchased at the price of the hurly-burly of daily life. This, however, does not lead into a crude pragmatism according to which the cash value of thought determines its truth. Life can be lived with a minimum of thinking. Routine can easily be substituted for reason. Many of our scientific problems never arise for the great mass of human beings. They arise within the sciences to which they are relevant. Solutions to them have the cash value only of producing greater consistency. But again, consistency is a feature of thinking, not of the world. People differ in their tolerance of obscurity and variety.

In the long run one can always say when one meets a difficulty, "This is the will of God," or, "Such are the facts." Nor is there any established rule in accordance with which one can tell when such tolerance is excessive. Novels like *Crime and Punishment, Mme. Bovary, Tom Jones,* or *Pride and Prejudice,* for that matter, are unscientific clarifications of individual events. The sharpness with which these events are depicted, not their inner consistency, is what turns into their "truth." Nor are the characters in these novels true as types of human beings; on the contrary, we often name the type after the characters. When we say that they are true to life, we surely do not mean that they are biologically true or psychologically true, for neither biology nor psychology deals with individual or unique events. The novelist creates a world and a kind of life into which his characters seem to fit since he gives us an insight into their minds which no simple observer on the outside could have. When he becomes scientific, he often becomes absurd. To realize this, one has only to recall the phrenological generalizations of Balzac. Fiction, which is a form of myth-making, is antiscientific in the sense that the better it is, by which I mean the more successful, the more individualized the characters are. This does not imply that they must be eccentric, but simply that they must be intelligible. They must establish in themselves a class of one member which is paradoxically enough human.

The sphere of reason is supposed to exclude all religion, all art, all the peculiarly human interests of mankind. But rationality is itself an aspiration and, I hope to have suggested, an aspiration guided by the very interests which it rejects. Reason is not religious, but the aspirations of the religious man impel the scientist toward his truths and the outcome of a science may be a form of religion. Reason is not an art, but aesthetic criteria are applied by the scientist when he tests his hypotheses, for what are simplicity and clarity if not aesthetic? But there is one peculiarity of reason which, as far as I know, is unique. Reason destroys accepted opinion and progresses over the dead bodies of its rivals. Renaissance art did not destroy medieval art nor did Roman art destroy Greek. As the Christian exegetes used to say, Christianity was the fulfillment of Judaism, not its destruction. But the truths of modern science contradict flatly the truths of Renaissance or medieval science. One can admire the art of a half dozen different periods and cultures and, what is more, one can understand and approve of it. One can admire the ingenuity of Aristotle's physical writings, but one can no longer accept them.

The question which is bound to trouble a modern man is whether the radius of the sphere of reason is expanding to the point where it will include all that is now included under the arts and religion. This seems to me to be unlikely, though I claim no prophetic gifts. It seems unlikely since reason always is propelled from behind and if the traditions of scientific method change, they will not change so radically that all metaphor, all myth, all concretions of ideas will have disappeared. For should that happen knowledge would be nothing but a notebook crammed with formulas which no one would either understand or be able to apply. Thought can never be so dehumanized that it contains no vestiges of its origins in human life. That moment will come only when our thinking machines begin to invent problems of their own.

Index